Go.AI
(Geopolitics of Artificial Intelligence)

By: Abishur Prakash

To my parents and my brother for their guidance and patience all these years.

Life Disclaimer

This book has a finite lifespan. The rate at which artificial intelligence is advancing and the number of new developments taking place mean that within a short period of time, this book will be irrelevant.

Table of Contents

Key Concepts & Definitions
...7-14

Introduction
...15-23

**Chapter 1
AI Espionage**
...24-39

**Chapter 2
AI Ethics**
...40-58

**Chapter 3
AI Mapping**
...59-76

**Chapter 4
AI Crime**
...77-94

**Chapter 5
AI Competition**
...95-113

**Chapter 6
AI Workers**
...114-127

Chapter 7
AI Bias
...128-142

Chapter 8
AI Policing
...143-161

Chapter 9
AI Trade
...162-188

Chapter 10
AI Education
...189-209

Chapter 11
AI Warfare
...210-233

Chapter 12
AI Politicians
...234-258

Conclusion
...259-271

Key Concepts & Definitions

For simplicity, this book does not go into the technicalities of AI.

When describing an autonomous weapon or predictive policing system, the term "AI" is used. However, AI is made up of many "moving parts". By understanding these parts, readers may be able to imagine new ways AI can be applied to geopolitics and other domains.

The moving parts of AI are explored below.

Broad AI Definitions

There are three broad categories that explain how AI is expected to evolve:

Artificial Narrow Intelligence (ANI): An AI system that can function with some degree of human intelligence.

Artificial General Intelligence (AGI): An AI system that can match all aspects of human intelligence.

Artificial Super Intelligence (ASI): An AI system that exceeds human intelligence.

Main AI Verticals

Within AI, there are three main verticals where most research and development is coming from:

Machine Learning: Machine learning is a type of algorithm that can learn from data and make decisions on its own. The more data that is fed into a machine learning algorithm, the more accurate and precise it becomes. An example of machine learning is the recommendation system that a US movie/TV streaming company has deployed. This system analyzes what a user is watching (data) and then makes recommendations about what he/she may want to watch next (learning from the data).[1]

Neural Networking: Neural networking is a sub-vertical of machine learning. The main difference between machine learning and neural networking is that neural networking systems are built differently. In neural networking, systems are modeled on the neural networks of the human brain. This allows them to learn in a more "natural" way. Neural networks are fed larger data sets and learn how to interpret these data sets without human input. It is machine learning but on a larger and more complex scale. An example of neural networking is a system that a US technology company has created. This system allows AI systems to constantly learn from one another and create more sophisticated neural networks.[2]

Feedback Loop: A feedback loop is a process through which AI demonstrates the work it has done so that the "work" can be approved or rejected. This allows AI to become smarter by constantly learning about where it has succeeded and where it has failed. An example of a feedback loop is a system that researchers at a US university have created. This system can predict cyber attacks with 85% accuracy. It predicts by looking through data and identifying "suspicious activity". It then presents this new data to a researcher who updates the AI with the correct and incorrect predictions.[3]

Generative Adversarial Networks (GANs): This is a sub-vertical of neural networking. Usually, neural networking involves a single system analyzing a data set and learning from it. With GANs, two neural networks are "pitted" against each other. One of the neural networks is called a "generator" while the other is called a "discriminator". The generator produces or passes judgment on a data set. The discriminator decides whether what the generator has produced/judged is right or wrong. An example of GANs is a system that a US chip company has created. These GANs can create brand new images by analyzing a single image. The system can take an image of a car driving on a rainy day and create a new image showing the same car, in the same environment, driving on a clear day.[4]

Deep Learning: In the same way that neural networking is a sub-vertical of machine learning, deep learning is a sub-vertical of neural networking. Deep learning is about two things: scale and type of learning. Until recently, the AI field had big ideas but could not test them because the computing power did not exist. Therefore, neural networking burgeoned as it mainly revolved around smaller data sets, which required less computing power (compared to deep learning). Now however, the computing power does exist and this is why deep learning is growing. While deep learning is about huge data sets (scale), it is also expected to allow more unsupervised learning at the same time. Today, the majority of machine learning falls under supervised learning. This means that data fed to an algorithm is labeled. For example, while teaching AI to recognize objects on a road, different signs will be labeled as "stop sign" or "yield". Or, if teaching AI to move emails into a spam folder, different emails will be labeled as "charity scam" or "fake bank alert". This allows AI to learn faster but it also restricts the AI from learning on its own and dealing with brand new variables and data sets. This is where unsupervised learning comes in. It is about AI interpreting a huge data set and connecting the dots on a massive scale, completely on its own. An example of deep learning is a system that can analyze silent videos and add sounds to them to accompany actions in the video, like banging on an object.[5]

Core Disciplines

While machine learning, neural networking, and deep learning constitute the three main verticals within AI, there are other disciplines that are also driving AI:

Brain-Computer Interface: This is the convergence of biology and technology. It allows someone to use their brain to control an object of some sort. The person sends a "signal" from their brain to an object to make the object behave in a certain way. The role AI plays is in converting the signal into actions. An example of a brain-computer interface and AI is a system that a Japanese music equipment company created. In an experiment, the company placed electrodes on the body of a dancer. Then when the dancer moved, AI converted the movements into signals for a piano. In other words, the dancer was able to play the piano through movement.[6]

Facial Recognition: This is a type of "biometrical software" that can identify a person by scanning and analyzing their face. It does this by allocating "points" (known as nodal points) to a person's face to create a skeleton. This skeleton is then processed by the facial recognition software to generate a unique ID of a person that cannot be copied by anyone else. An example of facial recognition is the Shanghai subway station which uses facial recognition to scan and identify people.[7]

Image Recognition: Also known as machine vision, image recognition is the ability of software to identify an image or identify objects in an image. This technology underpins services that many Internet companies have deployed. Many social media companies use image recognition systems. These systems can scan a photo that a user uploads and make suggestions about who should be tagged in it.[8]

Natural Language Processing (NLP): This is the ability of AI systems to understand what a user is doing through natural language. An example of NLP is search engines which autocomplete search queries based on what a person is typing.

Predictive Analytics: This is the use of huge historical data sets to predict future events. Historical data sets are fed into an algorithm which then identifies patterns. The algorithm then analyzes a current data set and compares the patterns it found earlier. Subsequently, the algorithm makes predictions about what may happen in the future. An example of predictive analytics is a retailer that analyzes historical data to predict which goods it should stock and at what prices.

Reinforcement Learning: This is a specific way to create a machine learning system. Reinforcement learning allows a system to learn entirely on its own, instead of "controlling" how a machine learning system learns from data. Reinforcement learning is related to feedback loops as such that machine learning systems are "rewarded" when they get something right. An example of reinforcement learning is teaching a system how to play chess. Instead of telling a system how to play or what the rules are, the system is allowed to learn on its own. If the system succeeds and learns what to do, it is rewarded (its learning is then reinforced).

Voice Recognition: Also known as speech recognition, voice recognition is the ability of software to execute commands through vocal expression. Voice recognition exists in services like AI assistants which can execute voice commands like "Call Mom" or "Set a Reminder". But the next era of voice recognition revolves around integration with AI. The expectation is that future voice recognition software will be able to "interpret" what people are saying and execute more complex commands. An example of voice recognition/speech recognition is an API from an AI company in the US. The API allows smart assistants to feel the emotion in a person's voice.[9]

Introduction

The concept of artificial intelligence (AI) is quite old.

Greek myths speak of "golden robots", created by the Greek god of fire to serve him on Mount Olympus. Records from ancient China mention an engineer who gave a Chinese king an "automaton" that could walk and dance. Today, AI is not just for gods or kings. It is being created everywhere, for everyone.

An advertising agency in Japan employs a creative director for AI. Executives prefer AI-generated ads over the ones humans are producing.[10] In the US, a technology company's AI can make phone calls, and people on the other end have no idea they are talking to a robot.[11] In China, an e-commerce company has created AI for advertising. It can produce 20,000 lines for advertisements in a few seconds. [12] In Denmark, a startup is supplying AI to listen to emergency calls and tell if someone is having a cardiac arrest. [13] In the United Kingdom, an AI at a hospital can predict when people with heart failure will die. It has an accuracy of 80%, compared to a human doctor's accuracy of 60%.[14]

These examples are just the tip of the iceberg when it comes to what is taking place in the world of AI. But they communicate an important message: AI is set to transform the way the world works. In the future, AI could become so advanced and sophisticated that the advances of today would be akin to the "art" that cave men drew thousands of years ago.

As AI advances, it sparks debates and discussions. Most of them have to do with AI's impact on society and economy. Could AI be biased against someone because of their gender or ethnicity? Will AI benefit some economies more than others? Will AI give governments more control over citizens?

These questions are important. But there is more to AI.

One of the most seldom discussed areas, and the focus of this book, is the geopolitics of AI. As AI advances, it could change the balance of power around the world. It could influence relationships between countries, challenge global institutions and structures, and even drive peace and security toward unexplored avenues.

Until now, most conversations about the geopolitics of AI have been about one topic: war. That is, could AI break free and start the next world war?

The problem with looking at the geopolitics of AI in this way is that it makes it seem like there is nothing else. As this book will show, the geopolitics of AI is made up of so much more than autonomous weapons or killer robots.

This makes the following pages more like a map of the future. As geopolitics is transformed by AI, business executives, political leaders, and stakeholders around the world can use this book to navigate the unfamiliar.

It is important to note here that this book is not technical. A reader will not learn how to build AI and apply it to geopolitics. This book is about possibilities. This book is about the future. It is about lighting an area that has previously been dark.

The first chapter looks at AI espionage. One of the main ways in which people will interact with AI is through AI assistants. But depending on where these assistants come from, they may have ulterior motives. Countries could use AI assistants to expand their foothold in other countries.

The second chapter looks at AI ethics. To make AI behave a certain way, it is being loaded with ethics. However, ethics may differ from country to country. And this means AI could behave differently based on the ethics it has been loaded with. AI ethics could become a new source of tension between countries as AI makes decisions that other nations and societies do not like.

The third chapter looks at AI mapping. This is the use of AI to scan satellite imagery and make inferences about a particular country or region. As AI mapping is used, it could change how countries and businesses operate in foreign markets, antagonizing local governments. At the same time, AI mapping could mean countries no longer control their global reputation.

The fourth chapter looks at AI crime. A segment of organizations that may use AI is organized crime groups. As technology advances, it could reach a point where criminal networks use AI to execute entire crimes. This could create tensions between countries as citizens and societies are put at risk.

The fifth chapter looks at AI competition. As countries and companies deploy AI to manage operations, it could lead to different AI systems competing with each other. This means nations could be competing with each other through AI mediums. As AI competes, it could cause countries to clash with one another.

The sixth chapter looks at AI workers. As AI takes over all kinds of tasks and jobs,

AI systems could become the new workforce of nations. This is a new risk for countries as these workers could disappear or be manipulated. Economies could be put at risk if a company or country "pulls" their AI workers.

The seventh chapter looks at AI bias. Alongside biases that AI may have, like racial bias or gender bias, there could also be a "political bias". AI may have a bias toward another country because of historical conflict or current affairs. This could cause AI to make decisions that affect countries negatively.

The eighth chapter looks at AI policing. Thanks to AI, predictive policing (police predicting crimes before they take place) is becoming real. But predictive policing could lead to countries arresting foreigners and nations manipulating predictive policing systems to meet a foreign policy goal. Because of AI, policing could become a variable of geopolitics.

The ninth chapter looks at AI trade. Like with border control and security, countries may put AI in charge of trade. As AI manages trade, it could start to think about trade and trade deals in a brand new way, upsetting other countries. At the same time, as AI itself is traded between countries, it could be used to create brand new blocs.

The tenth chapter looks at AI education. In the coming years, people may begin to download skills and subjects instead of learning them. AI could be the backbone of this new era. As this revolution in education takes place, it could take societies into dangerous territory because of where the downloadable skills are coming from and what people are learning.

The eleventh chapter looks at AI warfare. The next version of missile defense systems, fighter jets, tanks and robot soldiers may be fully autonomous and self-thinking. This means AI could soon be in charge of military decisions, including engaging targets. As AI takes over warfare, it could threaten peace, security, and stability around the world.

The twelfth and final chapter looks at AI politicians. As people in societies all over the world become resentful toward human politicians and political systems, they may be inclined to vote for an AI system instead. As AI takes over politics, there are several ways it could affect geopolitics.

At times, this book may feel "out there". Even discussing something like AI-led education may seem more science fictional than real. But consider that every scenario in this book is based on real advances and research. This book applies what is already taking place to the world of geopolitics.

Equally important is that as one reads this book, they should not look at the geopolitics of AI through the geopolitics of yesterday. Any beliefs about previous eras of geopolitics must be suspended, if not fully discarded, to understand the book in its entirety.

To see how a natural gas shortage could affect European geopolitics, one can look to the past. But to see how an AI missile defense system could affect the Middle East, there is no precedent to fall back on.

The geopolitics of AI is brand new and different from anything that has come before it.

Moreover, unlike traditional geopolitical variables, such as oil or natural gas, which nations had to be lucky enough to have, AI is different. AI is not dug up from the ground, it is created. It is up to nations to decide whether they want to define AI or be defined by it. For the first time in history, the geopolitical destiny of nations is not based on what is in their borders, what has happened in the past or where they are located in the world. It is based on something within their control. All that is needed is ambition and vision.

Unlike other books on geopolitics, every chapter in this book is dynamic. Chapters can be blended with each other. Different concepts can be pulled out and switched between chapters. The countries mentioned in the following chapters can be replaced with different countries and yet end up with the same outcome. In the geopolitics of AI, there are no rules; there is no right or wrong. In the geopolitics of AI, the world is in a state of flux. And when the world is in a state of flux, anything is possible.

In 2017, to mark the beginning of the new school year, the president of Russia addressed students throughout the country. The president of Russia, a country with 140 million people, thousands of nuclear weapons, a dynamic economy and more resources than most of the world combined, said the following about AI: "Artificial intelligence is the future, not only for Russia, but for all humankind. It comes with colossal opportunities, but also threats that are difficult to predict. Whoever becomes the leader in this sphere will become the ruler of the world".[15]

These words, from the leader of one of the world's most powerful countries, point to AI as being a key. By possessing this key, countries could unlock a brand new future for themselves. Depending on the country,

AI may do different things. For one country, AI may unlock a cottage. For another, it may be a castle. AI will be relative and may change its form based on who controls it.

And that makes AI more akin to a biological organism than a technology. Like an organism, AI is evolving. Like an organism, AI is spreading. And like an organism, AI will affect every country differently.

Welcome to the geopolitics of AI.

Chapter 1
AI Espionage

Berlin, Germany
2039

In 2039, violent anti-government protests start in Berlin. Thousands of people take to the streets, damaging government buildings, looting banks, attacking offices and vandalizing property. Berlin comes to a standstill. Over the course of a few days, the protests spread to other German cities such as Munich, Hamburg, Frankfurt, and Cologne.

Caught off guard, Germany's main intelligence agency, the Federal Intelligence Service (FIS), begins investigating why these protests broke out.

After weeks of analysis, the FIS connects the violent protests to AI. For several months, an AI system had been generating fake news, misinforming the German people about what the government was doing. This provoked and sparked the protests. The AI was created by a US technology company which provides a range of digital services to German citizens.

The FIS also learns that this AI was hijacked by a US intelligence agency. This agency was behind the misinformation. By misinforming German people, the agency had hoped to influence the upcoming German elections.

The FIS briefs the German chancellor.

Fifteen minutes after the briefing, the US technology company is banned in Germany under espionage laws. At the same time, US diplomats are thrown out of Germany and the German ambassador to the US is recalled. Minutes later, the president of the United States calls the German chancellor.

Just as the two leaders begin talking, the head of the FIS walks into the chancellor's office with a shocked expression. The chancellor quickly puts the call with the US president on hold.

"It is much worse than we thought," the head of the FIS says. "It is not just the Americans who have been engaging in espionage through AI. The Brits have been doing the same. And there are initial assessments that Japan, South Korea, and Israel are also involved, each using AI to influence the German elections."

The German chancellor stiffens.

Multiple countries have been trying to meddle in Germany.

And they have been doing so in a way nobody expected: through AI.

Introduction

To gain an advantage over another country, governments have constantly engaged in espionage. Through espionage, governments have tried to gain critical information that can help them outplay another country. However, throughout the years, one factor has remained the same: espionage has always been carried out by humans. It has been humans recruiting other humans or humans switching sides or humans playing a double game.

As governments apply AI to geopolitics, it may change how espionage is conducted.

As AI advances, one of the forms it can take is as an AI assistant. Several AI assistants exist today on smartphones. However, these assistants are not very advanced. A user may be able to use an AI assistant to make a phone call, send a text message, or check the weather – but this is simply an extension of what a user can do with their phone.

AI assistants will truly matter when they start doing things that are not possible today.

For example, could an AI assistant produce news for a user? If there is an alert that Vietnam and Cambodia are in a standoff at the border, an AI assistant could write a brand new article for a user. It could create original content, including graphics, statistics and data. This article would be unique from any other article on the Internet. The AI assistant may even produce the article in a way that aligns with the users political, social, and cultural leaning.

Or, could an AI assistant act as a personal investment banker? By monitoring a person's bank account, along with stock markets, government policies, and economic changes, an AI assistant could create a personalized investment plan. The AI assistant may even predict what will take place next to maximize returns. On its own, the AI assistant may move money between accounts, negotiate new contracts with banks, take on credit and loans, or recreate entire investment portfolios.

These examples represent the true potential of AI assistants. This kind of functionality will give large portions of the world's population access to services they did not have before.

But as the world taps the potential of AI assistants, concerns may emerge about who is supplying these assistants and how these assistants are making decisions. They may be benefiting certain companies or acting in the interests of a foreign government. As AI assistants spread throughout the world, a new geopolitical challenge will emerge. They could be used as a tool of espionage. Governments could use AI assistants to collect critical information on countries in order to beat them.

Stopping Germany's Reorientation Through AI

Fake news terrorizes governments and people. The fear is that an adversary could create fake news to make people believe false information. This could affect society and its important events, like elections. If fake news manages to influence people, they may vote differently.

During the 2016 presidential elections in the US, the Republican candidate was a vocal critic of the media, accusing them of producing fake news to steer the election. In April 2017, the new US president skipped the White House Correspondents' Dinner and at a rally marking his first 100 days in office, he lambasted the media, telling them that they should receive "a big, fat failing grade".[16] At the same time, during the 2017 presidential elections in France, fake news accounted for 25% of all political links trending on Twitter in France.[17]

To curb fake news, organizations are turning to AI. In May 2018, a US technology firm announced it was working on algorithms to stop the spread of fake news on its search engine and networking platform.[18] In the same month, a separate US technology firm announced that it will be applying AI to its news service to crack down on fake content.[19]

However, it may be up to social media companies more than anyone else to crack down on fake news. Not only are many of these companies working on AI, but they have become the main way people read the news. For example, the largest social media company in the world, with more than 2.19 billion users, is the main way 44% of people in the US get their news.[20]

To combat fake news, a US social media company could launch an AI assistant named "Emily". People could use Emily in a variety of ways. But the most important feature of Emily may be its ability to create "personalized news" for people. Emily may be able to write stories that are unique for each user and tailored to meet the user's "tastes". Hundreds of millions of people around the world may use Emily to learn about what is going on.

There is another way to look at this. A US company could control the AI technology that billions of people around the world may be dependent on.

This could pose a geopolitical risk to countries such as Germany.

Today, a new world order is emerging, led by China, India, and Russia. It challenges the traditional world order that has led the world for centuries. For instance, this clash between the old and new heavily impacts Germany. German economy and businesses are becoming more and more China-centric. Soon, its foreign policy might follow the same direction. In the coming decades, as this "reorientation" of Germany intensifies, the US may want to keep Germany in its sphere of influence.

A service like Emily could be useful in accomplishing this. Emily could collect huge sums of information on Germany's population. The US social media company might know what Germans think, what their political beliefs and desires are, and what they plan to do in the next election. With this information, the social media company could have Emily produce news to "meet a certain goal", like swinging an upcoming German election in favor of a certain party. Will the social media company work alone or will the US government also support it?

If Germany finds out, the country may denounce this as a new kind of espionage. The US would be actively trying to change the outcome of the German election through an AI assistant influencing what people in Germany think.

However, this will not be the first time Germany would deal with espionage through technology. In February 2017, Germany's Federal Network Agency and the German regulator for telecommunications, energy and postal services banned a robot doll. They cited espionage concerns. The doll collected and shared all perceived data with a company in the US, a company whose clients include intelligence agencies.[21]

If Germany catches the US using AI to swing the German elections, it may fracture US-German relations. Germany may be forced to retaliate in an equally dangerous way. As of June 2018, the US-Germany relationship was already witnessing major changes, with the German foreign minister stating: "We can no longer completely rely on the White House...".[22]

Are the conditions emerging for a US-Germany showdown in the future?

To retaliate towards US AI espionage, Germany may also turn to its own AI.

Major German car manufacturers are speeding ahead in developing self-driving cars. Alongside the ability to operate without a driver, these vehicles could also perform tasks when the driver is not around. One of these tasks could be picking up groceries (this was proposed by a Swedish car company in 2014).[23] At the same time, major German retailers are opening up shop in the US and expanding throughout the country. One of them has said that their products could be as much as 50% cheaper than their US competitors.[24]

To strike back at the US, German intelligence agencies could hijack the AI in German self-driving cars. Germany could then program these cars to choose German retailers over American retailers. When German self-driving cars are directed to go and pick up items from a grocery store, these vehicles may pick German retailers instead of local US retailers.

As the US uses AI to disrupt German politics, Germany may use AI to disrupt US businesses.

How would the US react to Germany using AI in this way?

This is only one side of the coin.

The US and Germany are allies. If either country uses AI as a tool of espionage, it may fracture relations but it will not lead to war. But what happens when the country using AI for espionage is not an ally of the US or Germany? What if it was Venezuela supplying AI assistants to spy on the US or

Germany, for instance? If Venezuela is caught trying to swing an election or influence trade through AI, the US or Germany may throw diplomacy out of the window.

To protect themselves from foreign AI (working in the form of AI assistants or other AI services) governments may try to "vet" different AI systems operating inside their borders. In May 2018, the New Zealand government announced a new project to vet algorithms the government has deployed to make sure they are behaving fairly and ethically.[25] Is New Zealand trying to ensure AI behaves a certain way? What happens if New Zealand finds a major problem in the way a foreign AI system is behaving?

As governments seek to control how foreign AI operates, their motive may not be regulating bias or job losses, but to address their geopolitical concerns.

Controlling India's Economy Through Chinese AI

Fake news will bring its own challenges. But, AI assistants will go beyond just supplying information. Using these assistants, people will be able to conduct advanced tasks and this creates more geopolitical risks for nations.

Today, Western-oriented nations control the smartphone market. As non-Western smartphones make their way into markets around the world, worries may emerge as to how this foreign technology can be leveraged against a country.

Currently, China leads the growth of non-Western technology. India is a prime example of this. India is undergoing what is called a "smartphone revolution". In a country where the average price of a smartphone is $100[26], one country is behind the explosion of smartphones: China.

Data published in January 2017 reported on the market share of Chinese smartphone companies in India. While a South Korean company had the largest market share (22%), the next four leaders were all Chinese. 36% of India's smartphone market was controlled by just four Chinese companies.[27] In fact, the data from January 2017, was the first time that a smartphone company from India was not in the top five rankings.[28] Chinese smartphone companies essentially outplayed Indian companies in their own local market.

As people in India increasingly rely on Chinese smartphones, they may be introduced to Chinese AI, including AI assistants. Will these AI assistants be working to help users or will they be working under a strategy set by Beijing?

Consider that China has been working on its own AI assistants for several years.

In 2012, a trade alliance was formed in China. It was formed to compete with US technology companies who were making huge advancements in voice recognition.[29] In August 2017, China's largest search engine unveiled its own AI assistant. At the same time, the search engine company acquired a firm that will allow its AI assistant to reach markets outside of China.[30] In April 2018, a leading Chinese technology company unveiled an AI assistant to take on US technology firms in China.[31]

If tens of millions of people in India start using Chinese AI assistants, it could allow China to control India in a new way.

People in India may ask a Chinese AI assistant for news or information. Will the assistant produce news that makes China (and China's allies) look good? People in India may also turn to a Chinese AI assistant for e-commerce. The assistant could prioritize Chinese e-commerce companies over their Indian counterparts. Or, people in India could ask a Chinese AI assistant to manage their finances. The assistant could tap into Chinese finance companies over the ones in India.

As people in India access Chinese AI assistants, India may be witnessing a new kind of colonization taking place. Except, this time China could be using AI to colonize India!

There are several geopolitical implications here.

Firstly, what will China do with all the data its AI has access to?

China might decide to share it with its allies, such as Pakistan. China may share its data on India with Pakistan, giving Pakistan knowledge on what India's population is searching for and communicating about. This data could be very specific, meaning Pakistan could have data on individuals, not just on broad trends. New surveillance fears could surface in India and questions will emerge as to if Pakistan could use this data in a destructive manner. For example, through the data, China and Pakistan may be able to see that there is growing anti-government sentiment. Because the data may be specific to individuals, China and Pakistan may be able to see which people and groups are displeased with the government. If tensions flare with India in the future, could China and Pakistan quietly support these groups?

The second implication is whether China's economy will get a boost.

China will know what products and services are in demand in India in a way even the government of India may not know. China could use this to change the way it sells in India. For example, China could flood India with certain goods to beat local companies and dominate the market. Or, alternatively, China may cut supplies of certain goods that are in high demand. This would increase demand and raise prices, benefitting Chinese firms.

Lastly, how will India respond if it learns that China's AI assistants are behaving in this manner?

India cannot respond in kind, as Indian smartphones do not have the same reach in China as Chinese smartphones have in India. At the same time, the Indian government cannot recall all Chinese smartphones due to cost and logistics. China's AI assistants will force New Delhi to adopt a different strategy. One strategy India could adopt is to convince foreign smartphone makers to load Indian operating systems (OS) in smartphones – which may include Indian AI assistants. Ironically, it was unveiled in April 2018 that this is what Chinese firms are doing as trade tensions with the US grow – they are building their own OS for smartphones.[32]

By using Indian OS on smartphones, people in India would be using Indian "AI assistants", not AI assistants from China or anywhere else. Indian AI assistants would act in the best interest of India, supporting Indian businesses and institutions.

However, even this is not a permanent fix. What happens if India's AI assistants are hacked?

Conclusion

Today, espionage is defined in a certain way. An Israeli government employee gaining critical information and sharing it with Iran or a Russian general sharing sensitive war plans with the United Kingdom are examples of traditional espionage. As AI makes its way onto the world stage, it will not only change how espionage is defined, but how espionage is conducted.

No longer will people be the main way to collect critical information.

In the age of AI espionage, governments will have to devise a way to counteract nations who use AI to get the upper hand. Governments could try to vet what kind of AI is operating in their country or they could try to force their populations to only use locally made AI. Each of these strategies carries its own risks and rewards.

Perhaps the most pressing concern is what happens if a country actually succeeds in using AI as a tool of espionage. Because AI is not in plain sight, like a person or military base, countries may succeed with AI espionage for decades before they are caught. And in those decades, the country could procure all kinds of benefits and advantages for itself. The "victim" country on the other hand could lose out in ways that are unimaginable. In the future, a country's biggest geopolitical vulnerability may have nothing to do with energy or currency. It may have everything to do with how dependent the country is on foreign AI. How dependent a nation is on foreign AI could make the difference between independence and enslavement.

Chapter 2
AI Ethics

Dubai, United Arab Emirates
2026

In 2024, the United Arab Emirates (UAE) unveils a brand new AI strategy to become one of the top five leaders in the AI world. This new strategy centers on creating Emirati AI firms by turning each of the UAE's three main cities – Dubai, Abu Dhabi, and Sharjah – into AI hubs for startups.

Each city will focus on a different sector: Dubai will focus on finance and banking, Abu Dhabi will focus on entertainment and retail, and Sharjah will focus on environment and agriculture.

Within a few short years, the UAE's AI strategy starts to pay off.

In Dubai, several disruptive AI startups emerge. But before the UAE government allows them to sell into foreign markets, it forces them to program certain ethics into the AI. Because the UAE is an Islamic country, many of the ethics are derived from Islam and the Emirati culture.

One of the first markets the AI startups enter is France, a secular state.

Many French companies try the AI. It is free and has capabilities that other AIs do not.

However, France has an algorithm that analyzes foreign AI. As the algorithm analyzes the AI from the UAE, it finds that the AI has ethics that are Islamic. France tells the UAE to change its AI and remove the ethics as it does not want religious influence in any form.

The UAE refuses to change or remove its ethics. It is proud of its culture and heritage and wants its ethics to be used by France and the world.

To protect its secular society, France bans the AI from the UAE until the ethics are removed. At the same time, France's algorithm looks into AI services from Saudi Arabia and other Middle Eastern states. It finds similar ethics and bans AI from these countries as well.

The Middle East fumes.

For many Middle Eastern countries, AI has become one of their biggest sources of revenue.

The Arab League convenes over France's actions and gives France an ultimatum.

Let Middle Eastern AI in or buy oil elsewhere.

Introduction

Ethics has to do with what is right or wrong; with how one should behave in a situation where a lot is at stake.

An ethical exercise to test people with is the "trolley cart" scenario.

A trolley cart is speeding down a train track. A short distance away, the track diverges into two separate tracks. The trolley cart must go on one of these tracks. But either route will cause someone to die. Tied down on the left track is a young mother with a six-month-old baby. On the right track are three elderly men, also tied down. The carriage will hit one of these groups. But which track should the cart choose? What is the most ethical way to decide who dies? All kinds of answers exist. The young mother and child may have more life ahead of them. The three elderly men may have contributed more to society. But there is no right or wrong choice here. The point of this exercise is to demonstrate the complexity and confusion that exists in making decisions.

Until now, people have been in charge of making ethical decisions. But in the future, AI will be in charge of making these same decisions. As calls for AI to be loaded with ethics surge, what kind of ethics should AI actually possess?

42

AI ethics has several layers.

The first layer is of who should be developing the ethics.

Consider that human ethics have been culminated over a long period of time by a variety of cultures, systems, ideologies, and conflicts. AI, on the other hand, is being developed in a relatively short period of time, by a small group of companies and institutions. Will it be up to private companies to create ethics for AI? Does it make sense to allow a US, Chinese, Russian or Israeli company to develop ethics for AI that billions of people might use? Should governments play a role, and if so, what kind of role?

The second layer has to do with the behavior of AI.

Ethics will dictate how AI behaves. Part of this means making sure AI understands what it is doing. If a medical company builds an AI surgeon, this surgeon will need to understand the concept of death, from a human perspective. If the AI surgeon is operating and makes a mistake, it may only have a few seconds to fix the problem before someone dies. If the AI surgeon does not understand death the same way as a human does, the decisions it makes may be different. Could the patient die because of this? Will the medical company be blamed for programming poor ethics into its AI surgeon?

Ethics may seem philosophical and social. But increasingly, they will become geopolitical.

When AI misbehaves or breaks down in another country, the blame could fall on the ethics and where the ethics came from. This makes AI ethics more than just a business or regulatory decision. AI ethics could become a new kind of "export" from countries to the world.

Using Ethics To Balance Russia And Poland

The AI world is dominated by a handful of companies stretching from North America to Europe and Asia.

One of the biggest companies in the AI world is an American e-commerce firm. The AI from this firm is loaded into smart speakers and smart appliances. It allows users to perform all kinds of tasks, such as ordering a taxi, getting recipe ideas for dinner, preheating the oven, or having the AI act as a "personal trainer".[33] As of February 2018, the AI was available in 38 countries. Some of them are in Eastern and Central Europe, including Poland, Slovakia, Estonia, and the Czech Republic. One country the AI was not in was Russia.[34]

In the coming years, the e-commerce firm may want to takes its AI into Russia.

However, the Russian government may be wary of letting the AI operate in Russia. The Russian government may be concerned that the AI will "interfere" in Russia. The government may also be worried over the lack of control it has over the AI. To address these concerns, the firm may program its AI to include ethics that make it "culturally sensitive". This is something a US technology services company has been working on. It wants ethics that will allow its AI to adapt to "cultural norms" and behave differently from country to country.[35]

Through ethics, the AI could behave differently depending on what country it is in. Ethics may decide how the AI behaves in two different countries, such as Russia and Poland.

In the future, that same AI may act as a historian. People could ask it to explain history.

People in Russia and Poland may ask the AI about a historical time period, such as the Cold War. And because of ethics, the AI may adjust the way it explains the Cold War in Russia versus Poland (cultural sensitivity). In Russia, the AI may speak of the success of the Soviet Union and how it had a positive impact on the world. However, in Poland, the AI may speak of the failures of the Soviet Union and the negative impact it had on Europe.

Through AI ethics, the US e-commerce company will be catering to the geopolitical desires of Russia and Poland. This would not be the first time that companies have done this. In March 2014, after Crimea joined Russia, a US technology company changed how its mapping service featured Crimea. Crimea was shown as "occupied territory" in the US, while in Russia, Crimea was simply shown as part of Russia.[36]

Through AI ethics, the US e-commerce company may succeed in Russia and Poland. But what happens if the AI messes up its ethics or acts in a way that is offensive to the government?

In Russia, the AI may explain the Cold War in a largely positive light. But when people ask about specific things, such as the Soviet Union's economic planning, the AI could present the Soviet Union negatively, for instance. The AI might say that the Soviet Union had extremely poor economic planning and this is what led to its breakdown in the 1990s. Whether or not this is true is irrelevant. What matters is whether the Russian government will be comfortable with AI from the US explaining the past in this way.

There is another way in which the AI could mess up because of ethics. The AI could start answering questions based on what the future looks like. While one set of ethics may control cultural sensitivity, another set of ethics may control how the AI includes the future in its answers.

For example, if someone in Poland asks the AI about the Cold War, the AI may answer based on what Poland's future looks like. The AI could predict that in 2033, the Polish economy will be 32% more dependent on Russia than it is today. Based on this prediction, the AI may feel that it is in Poland's interest to build stronger ties with Russia.

Then, when explaining the Cold War in Poland, the AI may talk about it more positively, to make people feel less hostile towards Russia. In Russia, the AI may include the future in its answers in a similar way. If people in Russia ask about the Cold War or about Poland's role in the Cold War, the AI could speak of Poland more positively. The AI may believe that it is in Russia's interest to have better ties with Poland because of what the future holds for the two countries.

Will Russia or Poland be okay with the AI answering questions like this? Russia and Poland will have to deal with an AI that answers political questions based on what tomorrow might look like.

If Russia or Poland feel that the way the AI behaves is a threat, either country (or both) may warn the US e-commerce firm. To quell fears, the US e-commerce firm may respond with an unconventional offer: allowing Russia and Poland to directly control its AI's ethics.

The US e-commerce company could offer Russia and Poland the ability to further change the ethics in its AI by aligning itself with what the particular government desires.

This is similar to what China has done with several foreign companies. When a US networking platform launched in China, it unveiled a Mandarin-language website that censors content the Chinese government does not want. [37] At the same time, a Japanese car company gave the Chinese government insight into how it runs its factories in China. [38] To operate in China, both companies changed their model to what the Chinese government wanted.

If Russia or Poland can change the ethics in the US-manufactured AI, it could alleviate any worries either country has regarding information being exposed to its people. By controlling the ethics in the AI, these countries may believe they control the AI itself. And it may work.

But this leads to a separate geopolitical challenge. If Russia and Poland start controlling the ethics in the AI, it could initiate a domino effect.

Other Eastern and Central European nations, such as Belarus, Lithuania, Ukraine, Latvia, Romania, and Moldova could begin calling for the same ethical control over the US e-commerce company's AI. At the same time, Asian countries such as South Korea, Taiwan, Bangladesh, Indonesia, Malaysia, and India may also call for the freedom to program ethics in the AI. These countries may similarly want to ensure their populations are receiving the "right" information.

If the US e-commerce company complies, governments may be manipulating history.

The AI may become extremely "culturally sensitive", and may describe history in different ways based on where it is operating. An explanation of the Soviet Union could render different results in Russia, Belarus, Poland, Kazakhstan, and Hungary. An explanation of World War II could render different results in India, Japan, South Korea, and Indonesia. This is akin to publishers making their articles and books different based on where they are being read in order to be "culturally sensitive".

What makes government control of AI ethics dangerous is the scale at which AI will be operating. Potentially, billions of people could be connected to some kind of AI in the future. When AI explains things differently because of ethics, it creates a huge division in the world based on what people believe and know.

It is not just history that governments may want to control through AI ethics. For decades, governments have tried to separate religion from politics. But increasingly, religious governments are coming into power. And, in certain countries, this means one religion is being pushed over others. Could governments use AI ethics to make a society lean more toward Christian, Islamic, Jewish, or Hindu values?

All of this means that AI ethics could be more effective at influencing what people think or believe than any school system, business environment, or government propaganda that has existed in the past.

Where Ethics Themselves Could Come From

Another geopolitical challenge around AI ethics is the origin of the ethics themselves.

Ethics will be rooted in the culture, society, ideology, history, and politics of a nation. And because each country has a different makeup, ethics could differ widely from country to country.

This division in ethics could cause new geopolitical tensions.

For example, alongside established AI powers like the US, China, Japan, South Korea, and Israel, there are countries that are trying to make a name for themselves in the AI world. One of these countries is the United Arab Emirates (UAE).

In October 2017, the UAE appointed the world's first minister of AI.[39] By 2030, the city of Dubai wants robots to account for 25% of its entire police force.[40] And, by 2057, Abu Dhabi's police force wants robot ambulances, self-driving police cars, and robot police officers (not to mention "genomic police").[41]

The UAE is establishing AI at the center of its society and future. In the coming years, the UAE may have other objectives. One of them could be to have UAE-based firms selling AI services around the world. The UAE may want to supply its AI to different countries. After all, which country's

AI is used will be a new indicator of geopolitical influence.

As AI firms spring up in the UAE, what kind of ethics will be loaded into their AI?

The UAE is an Islamic country based in the Middle East. Because of this, it is possible that the ethics will stem from their history and heritage. This means that AI firms in the UAE will be installing specific cultural and religious ethics into their services.

As people in other countries use Emirati AI, they may be exposed to this culture and religion in a new way. One country using Emirati AI could be France. However, France has always prided itself as being a secular country, unaffiliated with any specific religion.

Will France view the ethics in the UAE's AI as challenging France's secularism?

France may ask the UAE to change or remove the ethics from its AI-services. The UAE may refuse as it is proud of its culture and heritage. How serious will France view this? Will the convergence of religion and AI push France to take extreme action, like banning AI from the UAE? This may anger the UAE, who may be looking at AI to transform the economy and move away from oil. When the UAE's economy is put at risk because of an AI-ban, the UAE may take extreme action, such as limiting oil flows to France.

Ethics could cause a new "clash of cultures" as different countries/companies supply AI with ethics that other countries do not like or want.

Germany's Self-Driving Cars Face An Ethical Dilemma

The main reason to load ethics into AI is for AI to behave a certain way when lives are at stake. When AI ethics mess up and someone dies, the country where these ethics comes from could be held responsible.

In August 2017, an ethics committee in Germany unveiled the world's first ethics for self-driving cars. The German government said that it would be adopting these ethics. The ethics seek to ensure that people are protected as self-driving cars operate on roads. For example, the ethics require vehicles to value human life over other kinds of life, like animals. And, the ethics seek to ensure that if a human is hit, it is hit in the least damaging way. The ethics also specify that humans should not be judged by AI because of age, sex, ethnicity, and other physical characteristics.[42]

While this is a step in the right direction, how exactly will these ethics influence the behavior of German self-driving cars?

Over the next decade, Germany may export millions of self-driving cars to the US. As people buy these cars in New York, San Francisco, Chicago, Boston, and Los Angeles, eventually these cars will be put into an ethical dilemma.

For example, on a rainy day, a German self-driving car may be driving down a street in Manhattan. All of a sudden, the AI may realize that it has miscalculated its trajectory and cannot break fast enough to stop at the next red light. With the driver asleep, the AI will be forced to make an ethical decision. Does it jump a red light and smash into other vehicles? Or, does it smash into the corner of a building to save others but injure its passenger?

Ethics will decide what the German self-driving car does and such decisions will have an impact on US society.

People could be injured, or worse, killed. But for the first time, the accident and its aftermath will not be blamed on US drivers. It will be blamed on German AI. And when US investigators try to understand why the self-driving car behaved the way it did, they may blame German ethics.

If more accidents involving German self-driving cars take place, the US government will be forced to take action. Today, if a car is defective, US government agencies issue recalls or even bans. Will the US ask Germany to recall, reset, or recalibrate its ethics?

If so, it will mean the US is asking another government to change their AI ethics. At the same time, the US will be blaming Germany for the accidents. What will Germany do?

While Germany may feel pressured to change its ethics, the German government may not want to start a global trend. Germany may not want to start changing ethics for every single country that has a problem.

Germany might reject the demands of the US and take an aggressive stance to protect its ethics.

Being the largest economy in the European Union (EU), Germany might lobby the rest of the EU to adopt German ethics for self-driving cars. The EU could mandate that any cars that are imported into the EU must be loaded with EU ethics - originating from Germany. How would the US, Japan, China, and South Korea respond to this?

To ensure US car makers do not lose business in the EU, the US may initially comply with EU law. But, over time, the US may feel that by loading its vehicles with EU ethics, it is unable to grow its soft power.

Will the US call on the EU to allow US vehicles to have US-approved ethics? Or, will the US force all foreign automakers selling in the US to load their cars with US ethics? The US could take a more extreme approach and threaten to ban or tariff foreign vehicles if US ethics are not allowed. Today, the US threatens tariffs and bans over trade deficits. Tomorrow, the US may threaten tariffs and bans over ethical deficits.

AI ethics could fundamentally transform the relationship between countries as the ethics themselves behave in ways that cause danger and friction. At the same time, governments may view ethics as a prized export and something they seek to protect.

Conclusion

In the coming years, as AI spreads across the world, the way AI behaves will not just depend on public policy, infrastructure, or consumer preferences. Perhaps the most important factor will be the ethics that the AI is loaded with.

Ethics will be seen as a new way for governments to control AI, especially if the AI is coming from another country.

However, so far the conversation has been around AI ethics clashing with people.

But what happens when AI ethics clash with one another?

For example, if a German self-driving car is driving down a street and a Chinese self-driving car is driving on the opposite side of the street, both of these vehicles may have different ethics built into them. At the same time, they may be able to communicate with each other in the same way self-driving cars could talk with traffic lights and retail shops. Now, if both of these self-driving cars are about to get into an accident with each other, they may communicate with each other to figure out what to do. But what happens if the German self-driving car tells the Chinese self-driving car to do something that goes against Chinese ethics? Or, what happens if the Chinese self-driving car tells the German car to do something, but the German car ignores this because it feels that its ethics are superior?

How various AI ethics behave with each other is just as important as how various AI ethics behave with people.

AI ethics will change how governments view AI. Ethics have never been created in such a short span of time. Even human ethics have taken hundreds, if not thousands of years, to become what they are today. And over that time, there have been many errors and lapses in judgment that have taken place.

This makes AI ethics all the more dangerous and unpredictable.

Unlike wars or protests, which are widely reported, mishaps by AI ethics may be harder to notice. A self-driving car crashing into a park, a factory worker killed by an industrial arm, or an elderly couple chased by an autonomous drone, may seem scattered and disconnected.

But they can be linked together by the failure of AI ethics.

If ethics are to be blamed, then the companies and countries that created them are to be blamed. And if this happens, then as AI fails or messes up around the world, the social, cultural, political, and economic history of a nation may also come under question.

Chapter 3
AI Mapping

Washington DC, USA
2029

In 2026, a major recession hits China. It surprises most governments and businesses.

US multinationals declare huge losses. At the same time, the US stock market crashes. This forces the US government to intervene. To help US multinationals recover, the White House announces a $300 billion investment scheme.

The scheme will see the government invest $300 billion in select US multinationals. In exchange, the US government will get a board seat and a percentage of the stock. For the first time in recent history, the US government will be a stakeholder in some of its largest companies.

By 2028, the effects of the recession have disappeared. US multinationals are growing. But Washington hasn't forgotten the recession in China. It caught the US off guard. And this happened because the US was depending on Chinese government data to assess the Chinese economy.

The data was flawed, manipulated, and corrupt. It endangered the US.

In 2029, the US government launches a new AI mapping service. This service taps US satellites and generates satellite imagery every day on dozens of countries around the world. AI then analyzes the satellite imagery and calculates the health of the economy, watches for intellectual property theft and more.

The US directs the companies it invested in to start using its AI mapping service for China.

As US multinationals begin to use the AI mapping service, their decisions in China change. A US consulting firm stops construction of its new offices in Shanghai, Shenzhen and Guangzhou. A US technology firm cuts orders from Chinese suppliers by 30%. And a US financial services firm halts all of its operations in China. The AI mapping service shows companies a different face of China.

For example, the AI alerts the financial services firm that over a dozen Chinese government officials were working as employees. AI monitors the movements of these employees and finds that they were constantly entering government compounds after work. They were hiding their true identify and stealing intellectual property.

The US starts supplying its AI mapping service to the UK, Japan, and South Korea. Slowly, businesses around the world start to change what they do in China.

China grows furious at the US. Because of AI, China no longer controls the image of its economy and society.

Introduction

How does a country find out what is happening in another economy or country?

Today, to understand how the manufacturing sector in an economy is doing, organizations can turn to the "Purchasing Managers' Index" (PMI). This index tracks five variables, such as inventory levels, new orders, and deliveries.[43] A PMI score that registers above 50 means that the manufacturing sector is growing, while a score below 50 means the sector is becoming smaller. Through a PMI, an organization can gauge how healthy the manufacturing sector is in an economy.

But a PMI has inherent risks. What happens if the data used to create a PMI is wrong or if the government supplying the data is purposefully manipulating it?

To overcome these risks, a new solution is emerging to track what is taking place around the world: AI mapping, whereby algorithms analyze satellite imagery and identify how a particular area is changing.

This technology is already being put to use.

In February 2017, a US hedge fund told its clients that they should start looking at satellite imagery to gauge the state of China's economy. The main concern of the hedge fund, and many other organizations, is that the data coming out of China is not accurate.[44] By relying on government data, investors could have an inaccurate picture of China's economy. Almost a year before the hedge fund's recommendation, in March 2016, a US startup launched an index called the "China Satellite Manufacturing Index" (SMI). The index analyzes satellite imagery of over 6,000 industrial sites across China, containing 2.2 billion satellite observations collected over the span of 14 years. An algorithm is then applied to this data to identify patterns.[45] For example, has there been a drop in the number of trucks entering and leaving a factory? Has pollution dropped in a certain industrial site? Either change may indicate less production. As the SMI crunches more data, it generates a new picture of China's economy that businesses have never had access to before.

As AI mapping makes its way around the world, it could change how countries control their "image". Countries and companies turning to AI to gauge the state of an economy (or other aspects of a country) could aggravate local governments. Businesses could change their investment decisions or governments could change their foreign policy based on the picture AI creates.

New Tensions Between China And The US

In mainland China, surveying and mapping data is tightly controlled and requires strict approval from the Chinese government. Without government approval, private companies cannot engage in surveying or mapping (this has been illegal since 2002).[46] This is why digital maps of China have all kinds of discrepancies. Mapping companies cannot map China the same way they can map the US or Australia. Over the years, several organizations have been fined or investigated by the Chinese government for their mapping efforts. For example, in 2013, Beijing launched an espionage probe against a US beverages company for what they claimed was illegal mapping of "sensitive areas" in the country (specifically the Yunnan Province, located in southwestern China). [47] Years earlier, in 2009, two students and a professor from a British college had their GPS devices taken from them by Chinese police. They had collected information on 6,000 different geographic points, including areas rich in resources.[48]

How China behaved with the beverage company and college students shows how important mapping is to the government. China wants to control this, and until now, it has been able to because most mapping/data collection has taken place within China. But what would have happened if instead of sending people into China, the beverage company developed or bought AI mapping capabilities? The beverage company would have been able to map China from outside of China.

This is a marked difference from the past. And it means that China will have to deal with AI mapping influencing business decisions, which in turn may affect China's economy.

For example, should a US fast food company apply AI mapping to China, the AI might monitor malls and shopping areas in Beijing, Shanghai, Shenzhen, and Hong Kong. The AI might tell the fast food company that there is a 23% drop in the number of people in malls and shopping areas. The AI might say this is because there is a slowdown in the Chinese economy and people are becoming frugal with their money. Based on this insight, gained through AI mapping, the fast food company might then make different business decisions in China, like finding new partners outside of China, prioritizing other markets or cutting investments in the country.

From China's point of view, AI mapping could pose a serious risk to how businesses operate in the country. More important than anything else, AI mapping could pose a serious risk to optics.

A US fast food company deciding to use AI mapping is one thing. But what happens if the US government encourages its multinationals to use AI mapping for China, the same way the US hedge fund encouraged its clients? Washington may do this on purpose, to compete with China. And China would be forced to respond.

In November 2017, a team from a university in the US unveiled an AI system that can tell whether a neighborhood is majority Democrat or Republican. The team found that a neighborhood with more pickup trucks had an 82% chance of being Republican while an area with more sedans had an 88% chance of being Democrat. [49]

Such a grassroots understanding about politics in the US could help foreign governments "influence" US elections.

In the past, countries turned to donations or blackmail to influence elections abroad. Going forward, countries might turn to AI mapping. In a future election in California, China could identify which candidate it wants to win. Then China could use AI mapping to identify the neighborhoods it needs to "spin". Once these neighborhoods are identified, China could direct cyber soldiers to influence voters through social media campaigns, fake news, and emails. China could use AI mapping to influence US elections, the same way the US may use AI mapping to influence China's economy.

What will China-US relations look like if both countries are using AI mapping in this way? Thanks to AI mapping, countries may gain an unprecedented "awareness" about another country. This could create new distrust and paranoia between countries.

It is also important to consider the role that public policy could play. Certain laws could force organizations to turn to AI mapping. For example, in April 2017, the Chinese government unveiled draft laws that require companies, who collect data in China and export it, to undergo an "annual security assessment". This assessment, which specifically mentions economic data, would ban the export of data that, among other things, harms "national interests". [50] In China, data that harms national interests may be anything that hurts China's image of a rapidly growing and healthy economy. China's public policy around data sharing will make it even harder for foreign companies and governments to trust data supplied by the Chinese government.

This creates a new opportunity for AI mapping to flourish.

Tracking National Security Threats

In April 2017, the US Pentagon announced "Project Maven". This is a project, led by the Pentagon's Algorithmic Warfare Cross Functional Team, which applies AI to drone footage. AI then creates actionable intelligence for the Pentagon to use. An estimated 95% of footage collected by US drones is of the Islamic State (IS) operating in Iraq and Syria. The hope is that the AI will identify new threats and changes that human analysts may overlook or take too long to find.[51]

As governments deploy AI mapping to track changes in battlefields, governments may also use AI mapping to identify new national security risks.

In May 2017, a group linked to the IS took over parts of Marawi City, located in the southern Philippines. An estimated 85,000 people fled to emergency shelters, and the Filipino government announced martial law for 60 days in Mindanao, the island where Marawi City is situated.[52] In June 2017, the Philippines, along with Indonesia and Malaysia, began joint patrols of areas around Marawi City to stop the movement of radicalized soldiers. The Malaysian government voiced their fear that any crackdown on Marawi City could force the IS soldiers to move to Sabah, an eastern state of Malaysia.[53]

Could AI mapping help the Philippines, Indonesia, and Malaysia deal with IS militants?

AI mapping could track areas where IS militancy is on the rise. Once the AI finds something, it can inform the government. Perhaps, it will even alert the government in advance, making predictions as to what could happen.

This leads to several geopolitical grey areas.

First, which AI mapping service will countries such as the Philippines, Malaysia, and Indonesia use? Supplying AI to different countries is a new variable of geopolitics and so several nations may approach the Philippines, Malaysia, and Indonesia. Perhaps India will succeed, offering a cheap and effective AI mapping service. This means that through AI mapping, India will be building strategic military ties in Southeast Asia. How will India's adversaries and competitors feel about this?

Secondly, how will countries deal with the predictions AI mapping makes? For example, India's AI mapping service could predict that IS militants will move from the Philippines to Malaysia in a short period of time. Both the Philippines and Malaysia may be alerted to this prediction. But the Philippines may ignore this prediction, as it believes it has the situation under control. Malaysia, on the other hand, may believe what the AI is predicting and will not want IS soldiers coming from the Philippines. If Malaysia feels the Philippines is not taking appropriate action, Malaysia might take its own unilateral action. Will Malaysia enter Filipino waters or land and shoot the terrorists? Or, if the terrorists do pass through and cause chaos in Malaysia, will the Malaysian government go so far as to accuse the Philippines of supporting terrorism in Malaysia?

Each of these possibilities has its own, complex geopolitical web that is spun together by AI mapping.

While AI mapping may allow countries to deal with national security risks in a new and powerful way, it will also give certain countries a new way to expand their influence.

One of these countries could be Russia.

In March 2016, Russia signed a series of security agreements with Algeria to help them deal with IS militants. The agreements included the delivery of Russian satellite imagery on "key border crossings".[54] Thanks to the imagery, Algeria was able to thwart several terrorist threats. Tomorrow, Russia may deploy AI to the mix to create a powerful AI mapping service for Algeria and other countries. In fact, Russia may already have the AI. In January 2016, Russia's Ministry of Ethnic Affairs announced that they had developed software that uses AI to detect ethnic conflicts at an "early stage".[55] Could Russia apply this AI to its satellite imagery to detect terrorist threats at an early stage?

By supplying AI mapping, Russia could become one of the main intelligence providers in North Africa. And when Russia's AI senses a threat in Algeria or elsewhere in Africa, Moscow can go beyond supplying AI and offer a helping hand, such as selling Russian arms, military hardware, training local armies or even establishing a Russian military base.

Through AI mapping, Russia will grow its footprint and influence in Africa in a brand new way.

Could Terrorists Acquire And Use AI Mapping?

Increasingly, worries are growing over AI being armed or falling into the wrong hands. This extends to AI mapping.

In January 2007, Iraqi insurgents were caught with satellite images of British military bases. The images were detailed, showing vehicles, tents, and restrooms. It prompted the British government to raise the issue with the US technology firm behind the satellite images, which replaced them.[56]

In 2007, terrorists were using satellite imagery to plan attacks. In 2027, could they use AI mapping?

A future terrorist group may use AI mapping to gain unprecedented knowledge on the movements and capabilities of a target location, such as a military base. AI mapping in the hands of terrorists may predict events, like a day when the security will be lower due to weather or when a high-valued target could be present. With AI mapping, terrorists will have insight and accuracy they never had before. However, before terrorists can use AI mapping, they will need to acquire the AI mapping capabilities. Where might they get it?

One place could be the dark web, the part of the Internet where 99% of the Internet actually exists. The dark web is dangerous, as it offers people the ability to buy everything and anything, from arms to assassination. In the future, could it offer sophisticated AI, such as AI mapping? If so, today's fears of black markets fueling drug trade and trafficking may be replaced with new fears of the black market fueling dangerous AI systems.

Identifying New Resources, Creating New Competition

Another powerful application of AI mapping is with resources.

In January 2018, a US semiconductor company announced that it was working with NASA to map the moon and find resources. NASA supplied 50 years of imagery on the moon. The semiconductor company applied AI to crunch the imagery to find craters where resources are likely to be present.[57] Alongside this, in June 2017, a US technology firm launched a new program to apply AI to the environment. One of the projects under this program seeks to map land and "manage natural resources".[58] In other words, AI will map an area and help find resources.

Could AI mapping help find fresh water, one of the world's most coveted resources?

Countries like India, China, and several countries in the Middle East are all suffering from water insecurity. Only a few countries, like Israel and Russia, have developed advanced desalinization technology. Unless desalinization technology is democratized, solving fresh water shortages will depend on finding new fresh water reserves. One country that is especially at risk is Saudi Arabia. Within the next 13 years, groundwater will run out in the country. In February 2016, the Saudi government began taxing residents for using water to reduce waste and raise new revenue.[59]

In the future, instead of turning to taxation, Saudi Arabia may turn to AI mapping. But instead of deploying AI mapping in Saudi Arabia, it may deploy it globally.

Saudi Arabia could launch dozens of satellites for its AI mapping service. These satellites could scan and analyze areas all over the world to identify new, untapped water reserves. What happens when Saudi Arabia's AI finds reserves?

Saudi Arabia's AI may identify (or even predict) that there are fresh water reserves off the coast of the Netherlands. Naturally, Saudi Arabia will want to tap these reserves. To do this, Saudi Arabia might take a radical approach and claim ownership of them - a "finders keepers" approach. This may seem unconventional, but consider that fresh water will be so sought after that it could push governments to do and say things they may never have done or said under "normal" circumstances.

Alternatively, Saudi Arabia could inform the Netherlands about these fresh water reserves to access them. Saudi Arabia may even pay for access or propose an "oil for water" trading model (the Netherlands trades water, Saudi Arabia trades oil). But what if the Netherlands refuses to share the fresh water reserves with Saudi Arabia and instead drills and extracts the water for its own use? Saudi Arabia may be furious as its AI mapping service found the fresh water reserve in the first place. This could lead to new geopolitical tensions between Saudi Arabia and the Netherlands.

A bigger geopolitical challenge emerges if Saudi Arabia's AI identifies untapped fresh water reserves that are not on land, but in the middle of an ocean. For example, in 2013, huge fresh water reserves were identified off the coast of South Africa.[60] What if Saudi Arabia's AI had found these reserves or predicted their existence?

Saudi Arabia may have quietly sent vessels and built infrastructure in the area to extract the fresh water. But what Saudi Arabia is doing is unlikely to go unnoticed. Other countries might also predict water in the area or follow Saudi Arabia's lead. Will Saudi Arabia share the "loot" or will it fight to keep the fresh water its AI has found?

Applying AI mapping to resources could create the next geopolitical spat as countries demand access to resources they have found or restrict access to resources they want for themselves.

Conclusion

One of the most powerful professions is that of a cartographer. Cartographers decide what the world looks like. As cartographers draw different regions and geographies, they effectively control how people, businesses, and governments view and understand the world.

This is one of the reasons why there is growing debate over which world map to use.

For many years, the world has used the Mercator Map, which shows countries differently based on how close they are to the poles. However, the Mercator Map results in Western nations looking significantly larger than what they really are. To change this, calls are growing to use the Gall-Peters Map, which is far more accurate, but results in Western nations looking significantly smaller to their Asian and African counterparts.

This debate, over which map to use reflects the challenges of AI mapping.

AI will be the next cartographer, creating the next maps. But whose maps will the world use? And how will the world use maps created by AI? The maps that AI creates, of an economy or geography, may be what future generations and businesses use to understand the world.

AI mapping will change how the world is perceived. And as this happens, it will change how countries perceive each other. And when countries have a different perspective on one another, it will change how they behave with each other.

Chapter 4
AI Crime

Bangkok, Thailand
2037

Two weeks after being laid off at a factory, a Thai father wakes up to a text.

"Kidnap Samantha Cole and Steve Bowles. They are staying at the Hilton Hotel in Bangkok. A black van with the license plate 98-4467 is waiting two kilometers east of the hotel in a parking garage at the Siam Discovery Mall. All tools needed for the kidnapping are in the van. Once kidnapped, text this number for where to take them. You will receive 1 million baht. Reply YES if you accept".

The father is not surprised by this text. Some of his unemployed friends have received similar texts and many of them have done what the text asked. The father looks at his children, sleeping soundly. Having 1 million baht will put them through school and help pay for the house. The father looks at his phone and replies, "YES".

Later in the day, Samantha Cole and Steve Bowles disappear. Both Samantha and Steve are US citizens. This prompts the US embassy in Thailand to get involved. This is the 17th case of US citizens going missing in

Thailand in the past six months. Thai police raid the homes belonging to gang members associated with kidnapping but find no leads.

That is because it is not the gangs responsible for the crime. AI is.

For several years, a criminal organization in Europe has been using advanced AI to carry out crimes. The AI identifies victims, plans how to carry out the crime, and then executes the crime. It was this AI that tracked Samantha and Steve. It knew they were vulnerable based on what they were posting online. The AI disguised itself as a tour guide who would pick them up from their hotel.

But finding people to carry out the crimes was the most effective tool the AI had.

Because millions of people in Thailand are losing their jobs to automation, AI starts to "crowdfund" the crime. The AI contacts people who are likely to commit crime and take the money without asking questions. The AI had identified the Thai father as having no money and no job.

The kidnapping of Samantha and Steve is just one crime the AI had planned for the day. Another 35 crimes are scheduled to take place in Bangkok, Jakarta, Hanoi and other cities throughout Asia.

Around the world, governments are struggling to stop this new wave of crime. Crime committed by humans is one thing. Crime committed by AI is something else.

Introduction

Traditionally, crime has been perpetrated by people. People have killed or stolen throughout centuries. In the future however, people will not be the only ones committing crimes. AI will be as well.

There are already several instances where robots have committed "crimes".

In June 2015, a robot killed a worker on the floor of a factory in Germany.[61] In July 2016, a baby was run over by a security robot at a mall in California.[62] In November 2016, a robot ran through a glass wall and injured a man during a technology conference in China.[63] In March 2017, a robot hit a woman in a factory in Michigan, breaking her skull and killing her.[64]

In these examples, robots were not intentionally hurting people. These were sporadic, isolated events where technology malfunctioned. But in the coming years, AI could reach a point where it could be used to drive crimes. It could be used to intentionally hurt people.

As AI advances, one group that may turn to it is organized criminal networks.

Organized crime has always existed in some form, but never has organized crime been so vital to the way the world functions. For example, during the Great Recession, drug money was the only "liquid capital" for financial institutions.

An estimated $352 billion of drug money was "absorbed" by the global economy during the recession, more than the entire economy of Hong Kong. [65] Organized crime has become so profitable that in some cases, the revenue of organized crime groups exceeds that of the largest multinationals. In 2013, the revenue of a mafia group based in Southern Italy was €53 billion.[66] This was more than the revenue of the world's largest restaurant chain and the largest bank in Germany, combined. The mafia is also structured like a multinational. It has 400 "key operatives" (executives) that manage a global "workforce" of about 60,000 people.

As organized crime posts revenue in the tens of billions, AI may be the key to making the next $50 billion or $100 billion. At the same time, AI could allow organized crime to expand into new markets and evade police in new ways. As AI manages crime, it could create new challenges for governments. The safety of citizens and businesses could be put at risk. Because of AI, many types of crime could become geopolitical challenges for countries.

AI Could Kidnap Australians In Southeast Asia

Southeast Asia is a global tourist hotspot. Countries like Indonesia, Thailand, and Singapore receive millions of tourists every year. In 2016, Bangkok became the most visited city in the world with more than 20 million visitors, beating London and Paris.[67]

One group that makes up a huge number of tourists in Southeast Asia is Australians. Between June 2009 to June 2010, Australians made 6.8 million trips overseas, with Southeast Asia accounting for 53% of these trips.[68] 900,000 Australians travel to Thailand alone every year.[69]

As Australians travel to Southeast Asia, crimes against them are rising. Between June 2014 and June 2015, the Australian Department of Foreign Affairs and Trade (DFAT) reported 109 deaths of Australian citizens in Thailand.[70] While the main cause of death is drowning, other risks, like terrorism, are on the radar of authorities. In April 2017, Australia warned its citizens of a kidnapping threat in the Philippines as Islamic State (IS) extremism grows.[71]

As more Australians travel to Southeast Asia, organized crime may use AI to target them for crimes like human trafficking or organ trade. And AI could do this in ways governments are not prepared for.

To start off, AI could track Australians by monitoring their social media activity. The AI could look specifically for geotagging information, which is personal information embedded in photos and videos people upload. In May 2010, researchers published a report showing that they were able to find the home addresses of people who posted ads on a website even though these people had not shared their addresses publicly.[72] In December 2014, an Islamic State (IS) soldier published dozens of posts on social media that accidentally included his location through geotagging. An intelligence group watching this was not only able to find the town he was in, but the exact house he was living in.[73]

As AI tracks Australians through social media, the AI may also be advanced enough to learn about the "personality" of a target. In September 2017, researchers at a university in the US showed off an AI system that can tell a person's sexuality by scanning a few pictures.[74] In April 2018, researchers from universities in Austria and Germany unveiled AI that can tell what kind of a personality somebody has by tracking their eye movements.[75]

Alongside all of this, the AI may also try to hack into the personal accounts of targets, such as their email or credit cards, to spy on their communications and transactions. Once again, the AI would be trying to find out where targets are or where they plan to go.

With all of this information, the AI could begin ranking people based on how vulnerable they are to being kidnapped. Three male friends, traveling to Bali, staying in a cheap hostel, posting pictures in underground clubs or a newly-wed wife who is touring Kuala Lumpur on her own as her husband attends meetings, are all examples of the variables AI may look at when ranking people. Then the AI could alert locals to kidnap these people. In this scenario, AI would be driving the entire crime, from identifying people to monitoring them and then alerting criminals when the time is right.

AI that can find people already exists. Except criminals are not using it, law enforcement is.

An organization tasked with identifying and extracting children who have been forced into sex trafficking rings has been using AI, supplied by the US Pentagon's Defense Advanced Research Projects Agency (DARPA). The AI monitors the Internet differently from other software. Traditional AI does not pay attention to the same information that DARPA's AI does. For example, DARPA's AI will monitor a sex ad and look at things like price changes, the number of sex ads uploaded by a single user, and the description of the ad itself. Based on these variables, DARPA's AI can start modeling who the sex trafficker might be.[76]

If organized crime turns to AI to target Australians, it will create a brand new reality. For the first time, AI will be jeopardizing the safety of Australians. And this will force the Australian government to take action. But unlike in the past, when Australia could exert pressure on governments, who in turn exerted pressure on criminals, the real criminal is no longer people. It is AI.

One country where AI may target Australians is Thailand.

Initially, Australia and Thailand may try to counter AI crime by finding out which country the AI is operating in.

Suppose the AI targeting Australians in Thailand originates from Egypt. Does it mean that Egypt is responsible for the crimes in Thailand? Australia and Thailand could call on Egypt to take down the AI. However, Egypt may be unable to do so. The AI may be using Egypt as a proxy. Or, the AI may be supplied by a foreign company whose data servers are in Egypt. The company may have no idea its AI is being used by a criminal organization. This is a new risk for AI businesses: how their AI services are used by customers could be illegal.

If Egypt is unable to take down the AI, will Thailand temporarily block Internet connections from Egypt to protect Australians? Will Egyptian nationals undergo additional security checks when entering Thailand? These actions could create new tensions between Australia, Thailand, and Egypt.

AI crime will extend beyond borders and that means that what AI does in one country could affect many others.

If Australia feels that Thailand is not doing enough to protect its people, Australia itself could turn to AI. How might Australia do this? One solution is to create AI versions of Australian citizens. In July 2018, India announced that it was working on creating "cyber twins" of people through AI. These digital avatars would survive people after death and continue evolving, with unique thoughts and a complete personality. India is investing $1 billion to bring about cyber twins and other advancements.[77]

Like India, Australia could work on producing AI versions of its citizens.

By doing this, the Australian government might know how its citizens think. This could allow Australia to "predict" the decisions of its citizens traveling abroad. Alternatively, Australia's AI could simply look at social media and digital forums. Australia's AI, backed by the government, might also have access to more private information, like credit card transactions and intelligence information that may have been collected. Through all this, Australia could identify which citizens are most at risk of being kidnapped. Australia could alert and warn these people. Australian embassies could house these people or local police could be informed to pick these people up and protect them.

However, this raises two issues.

First, if Australia uses AI to protect its citizens in Thailand, the Thai government may see this as interference. They may see Australia's AI as challenging the power of the Thai police and unnecessarily scaring people, which in turn hurts tourism. This may offend the Thai government.

Secondly, Australia's AI might not just track Australian citizens. Other governments may ask Australia to also rank their citizens and help protect them. Countries like New Zealand, Japan, the US, and India might pay Australia for "AI protection". While Australia will be exerting its clout through AI, Thailand may see Australia's AI system as challenging the Thai government.

Crowdfunded Crime & Digital Currencies

As AI revolutionizes crime, it may also revolutionize who commits the crime.

AI could start identifying and finding people to commit crimes. These people could be ordinary locals who need work.

According to the United Nations (UN), within the next 20 years, over 50% of workers in Cambodia, Thailand, Vietnam, the Philippines, and Indonesia could lose their jobs to automation. This means 137 million people could potentially be unemployed in the coming decades. A percentage of these people will be in Thailand. And unless these people find work,

Thailand could have a pool of unemployed people measuring in the millions.[78]

An AI, seeing millions of unemployed people in Thailand, could start identifying Thai locals to commit crimes. It could contact them and offer them a sum of money to commit various crimes.

AI would start to "crowdfund crime". The AI may even identify people from outside a country to commit a crime, such as someone from Cambodia committing a crime in Thailand. Or, AI might bring in multiple people, from multiple countries, to commit a single crime. Again, this makes AI crime a cross-border challenge.

How will governments identify criminals if average workers suddenly change their behavior because of a text? How will police forces crack down on crime if millions of average people are potential criminals?

As AI drives crime, the monetary element will also create geopolitical challenges for governments. AI will be committing crimes to make money. And it will have to store this money somewhere.

In February 2018, Venezuela launched the world's first state-backed digital currency called "Petro". The goal of Petro is to bypass financial sanctions and sell oil in a new way. [79] For now, Venezuela controls who uses Petro. But in the future, to make Petro global, Venezuela may allow anyone to covert money into Petro. In a world where AI is driving crime, Venezuela could also be roped into AI crime. AI may be receiving payment in Petro and paying criminals in Petro.

If governments around the world find out that AI is using Venezuela's digital currency to carry out crime, it may start the next geopolitical spat between Venezuela and a range of countries. Will Venezuela change the model of Petro or will it ignore what nations are asking for? In the case of Australians being kidnapped in Thailand, geopolitics may decide how Venezuela responds. Could Venezuela ignore Australia, a calculated geopolitical response to allies of the US, whom Venezuela views as an adversary?

Digital currencies could play a huge role in AI crime. And if countries are behind digital currencies, like Venezuela with Petro, then countries could become accessories to crime taking place thousands of miles away.

Future Cyber Crimes Driven By AI

Alongside using AI to drive crimes like kidnapping, organized crime may direct AI to focus on a different kind of crime: cyber crime. In fact, because cyber crime takes place over the Internet, even small gangs and individual criminals may turn to it.

Already, cyber crimes account for more than 53% of all crime in the United Kingdom, and in the US, at least 50% of Americans have been hacked at least once.[80] The economic toll that cyber crimes will inflict will force nations to take extreme steps to protect people and businesses. For example, in 2015, the economic impact of cyber crime on businesses was estimated to be $400 billion. By 2019, this number is expected to cross $2 trillion.[81]

One way cyber crime could take place is through AI scamming. Unlike regular scams, AI will take scams to the next level. AI will have the ability to disguise itself as a person in a way that is indistinguishable from the real person. There are two ways AI will conduct scams: through audio and through video.

In May 2017, a startup in Canada unveiled an AI system that can mimic the voice of someone just by scanning their voice. The AI then applies its own filters and enhancements. [82] Alongside this, in July 2017, a video emerged of a former US president talking to a camera in the oval office of the White House. Except, this speech was fake. The video was real, but what the president was saying was from a speech he made several years ago. Through AI, the president was made to look like he was making that speech again in the oval office. The AI changed what the president was saying in the video to make it look like he was saying something he wasn't.[83]

Because AI can recreate videos and make people say things they have not said, future AI may also be able to create avatars of real people. AI could video-call someone and pretend to be a family member. The person receiving the call may not be able to tell if the person on the other end is AI or the real family member. Because of this hoax, they could end up doing whatever the AI asks, like sharing a password or transferring funds.

AI scams could create major challenges for governments as people and businesses lose money and fall prey to identity fraud. Could foreign governments deploy AI scams to hurt other countries?

In the future, a major crime wave could emerge in Vietnam. Tens of thousands of people and businesses may fall victim to AI that has disguised itself as a family member, a boss, a government employee, or a bank employee. Vietnam may panic as to how to respond. Upon further investigation, Vietnam may find that the AI committing these crimes has "fingerprints" from the Czech Republic. Will Vietnam accuse the Czech Republic of cyber crime through AI? Could Vietnam sue the Czech Republic in court to recover money that was stolen?

The Czech Republic however, may have no idea of what is taking place. It may be a small group of teenagers, in a rural part of the country, using cheap AI to scam people in Vietnam. How will the Czech Republic stop this if multiple gangs keep on using AI to commit these crimes? How will the Czech Republic build relations with countries when AI originating from the Czech Republic is attacking those same countries?

As AI scams scare people and businesses, governments could be blamed for failing to take action. And if governments blame each other, AI scams could start to affect the foreign policy of nations.

Conclusion

Most crime is not considered geopolitical.

Only certain types of crime is seen as geopolitical because of the cross-border or political nature of the crime itself, such as drugs moving across a border or the sale of weapons and arms.

These types of crimes and the challenges they create will not disappear.

However, what drives these and other crimes may change. In the future, people may take a backseat as AI drives crime.

AI entering the picture does not just change the way criminals conduct crime.

It changes crime itself.

What AI can do will be significantly more than what people can do. If AI starts to crowdfund crime, it redefines known theories and concepts about how crime begins, how to preemptively stop crime and who is responsible. Because crowdfunded crime has the potential to create chaos for societies, countries around the world may take swift action against the AI and the country responsible for developing it.

The greatest challenge of AI crime is whether it will lead to new forms of crimes. Just as automation is expected to take jobs and at the same time create jobs, so AI too could drive existing crime and also create new forms of crime.

If AI creates new crimes, such as new ways to hurt people or steal, it will jolt governments. Crime and geopolitics may become connected in a way they have not been before.

Through AI, local crime could become global.

Through AI, global politics could become local.

Chapter 5
AI Competition

Riyadh, Saudi Arabia
2034

Facing huge competition from renewable energy, Saudi Arabia announces that going forward, AI will be in charge of negotiating oil deals and selling oil on the global market.

Oil prices surge upward due to uncertainty. Investors and governments panic over how Saudi Arabia's AI will make decisions and what it will mean for the future of oil.

As Saudi Arabia deploys its AI, it also begins working with the Gulf Cooperation Council (GCC) to adopt AI for oil sales. In a span of six months, every country in the GCC has adopted AI, with the exception of Qatar. However, the GCC has an agenda with the AI. It wants to take on Iran. To do this, the GCC programs the AI to sell oil below $100. This will hurt Iran's economy as Iran needs oil to be at $130 to breakeven.

Iran, aware of what is taking place, also deploys AI to sell oil. However, thanks to nanotechnology and other industries, Iran is not as dependent on oil as it once was. To compete with the GCC, Iran programs its AI to sell oil below $50 - well below what most of the GCC needs to breakeven.

Through AI, the GCC and Iran are competing for oil sales.

In 2034, India announces that it wants to increase its oil reserves by 12%. At the same time, the country also announces that it will be buying oil through AI.

The AIs from the GCC and Iran snap to action.

Negotiations between GCC, Iran, and India begin. No humans are involved. The negotiations take place in seconds. Countries like Venezuela and Russia are cut out as they do not have AI to negotiate oil deals.

After a few minutes, the GCC and Iran receive a surprising response from India's AI: they have lost the bid. Scratching their heads, states across the Middle East try to figure out what happened. Did their AI make a mistake? Is India abandoning its oil reserve plan? Did geopolitics hijack their oil deal with India?

Little do the GCC and Iran know that as their AIs negotiated with India, another oil power also directed its AI to work with India. And this oil producer priced its oil at $30 to grow its energy power in Asia.

The oil producer was the US.

Introduction

When we think about AI services today, we think about services such as AI assistants on smartphones or AI that crunches huge amounts of data for businesses. These services come from different technology companies located around the world. For the most part, these different AI systems do not compete with one another. While the businesses may be competing with each other, the AI itself does not compete with another AI. For example, today if a smartphone user asks their AI assistant to explain what happened during the Cuban Missile Crisis, the AI assistant will search the web and distill the information it finds. The AI assistant will not be competing with another AI assistant from a different smartphone for access to information on the Cuban Missile Crisis. In the future though, things may be different. A smartphone user might ask their AI assistant to find and buy the best healthcare plan. As the AI assistant goes "into the market", AI systems from various healthcare companies might try to communicate with the smartphone's AI assistant. As AI systems compete with one another, it will spawn a new era of competition.

The foundation for AI competition already exists. In several instances, researchers have pitted AI systems against each other to study how AI behaves when it has to compete.

In a study published in February 2017, researchers looked at how bots behave as they edit content on an open encyclopedia. Researchers examined the bots between 2001 and 2010 in 13 different languages of the encyclopedia (English, German, Portuguese, etc.). What they found was that when two bots identified the same page to edit, they kept on "circling back", undoing the edit of the other or writing over it. The researchers said that this could be an "infinite loop" whereby the bots keep on forever changing what the other did. Furthermore, the study found that bots adapted to the culture they were operating in, with bots editing the German version of the encyclopedia being less aggressive than bots editing the British and Portuguese versions.[84]

In January 2017, a video stream was launched showing two modified AI speakers chatting about different topics, such as religion and love. Eventually, the two AI speakers began arguing with one another, with one AI speaker threatening to "slap" the other. [85] In September 2016, several technology companies participated in a gaming competition. Each company developed an AI to compete in a popular video game. In the first round, which had standard maps and configurations, AI from a social media company won 10 out of the 12 matches. In the second round, weapons were scattered throughout the game, requiring the AI to learn and adapt. In this round, AI from a semiconductor company won the round, winning 10 out of the 12 matches. One of the AI systems, developed by a university in the United Kingdom simply camped (stayed in one place) at different areas of the game where people would spawn (start off), mimicking a human tactic in gaming.[86]

As AI competition grows, it could become a new type of competition between nations. As different AI systems compete with one another, governments could be roped in and brand new geopolitical divisions could emerge.

US And Chinese E-Commerce Clash In Australia

In 2012, an author published a book online to help kids learn about computers. It was priced at $14. As sales picked up, the author noticed that his books were being sold for as high as $55 on some platforms. With more research, he found that it was not humans reselling the book at a high price, but bots who were competing with each other. These bots were buying the book for $14 and then reselling it at different prices, some as high as $55. As the bot competition intensified, the bots would then reduce the price of the book to undercut the other bots. A US e-commerce company ended up selling the book for less than anyone else, due its own bots partaking in the competition.

Bots scouring the web and indexing websites is not a new behavior. But AI identifying products autonomously, making decisions about what price point to resell the product at and then actively competing with other AI systems to achieve sales is a brand new phenomenon. And it could create new geopolitical tensions as competing AI systems create problems in countries.

In February 2017, the world's largest e-commerce company from China opened its first office in Australia, formally bringing Chinese e-commerce into the Australian market. Also present in Australia is the largest e-commerce company in the US. [87] Until now, these two e-commerce companies have not directly competed with each other. They have been limited to their respective markets. Now, in Australia they will have to compete head-on.

What makes Australia significant is that the country is at a geopolitical crossroads. They need the US for defense, but rely on China for economy. The competition between the two e-commerce companies could be the first indicator of which country Australia will lean towards.

One way the two e-commerce companies could compete is by deploying AI to bid on products, reduce prices and undercut the other with no limits, like a 40% reduction on a pair of shoes. As AI from China and the US compete with each other, to what extremes will these competing AI systems go to make a sale?

In February 2017, a US technology company unveiled that it had deployed two AI systems to play a fruit-picking game. The AI systems were equipped with laser beams to knock the other AI out. When there were lots of fruits, the AI systems played fairly. But when the number of fruits diminished, the AI systems became "highly aggressive" and used their laser beams against each other.[88]

Could the AI systems from China and the US also behave aggressively?

For example, the US AI system might begin creating fake news about China's e-commerce company. It could say that China's e-commerce company is selling fake leather labeled as real leather. Then, the US AI system could publish this fake news on social media. The AI could then create hundreds (or thousands) of fake accounts on social media and upvote the posts to make them go viral.

Now, as word begins to spread that fake leather is being labeled as real leather, China's e-commerce company may take a hit in Australia. In response, China's AI might snap to action. China's AI might start contacting suppliers in Australia, disguising itself as a representative from the US e-commerce company. It might tell the suppliers that all contracts are cancelled as the US e-commerce company is declaring bankruptcy. As news of this spreads, investors might start pulling their money from the US e-commerce company, causing the stock price to plummet.

As this AI competition continues, it will eventually reach a point where the Australian government will have to step in. The way the AI systems behave may breach anti-trust or anti-competition laws. The Australian government will have to take action, but against whom?

Australia's decision will have geopolitical consequences. If Australia sides with the US e-commerce company, China will not be happy. If Australia sides with China's e-commerce company, the US will not be happy. AI competition could put Australia in an awkward situation. AI competition could force Australia to pick a side at a time when Australia might not want to.

Jumping Into Middle Eastern Commodities

Companies may decide to deploy AI to help them compete in sectors like e-commerce and retail, but countries may deploy AI to help them compete in areas like commodities. Once again, this has consequences for geopolitics.

In May 2017, a think tank from the United Kingdom warned that oil prices could drop to $25 a barrel in the coming years as new technologies emerge, like self-driving cars.[89] Oil reaching $25 will create huge political and economic challenges for oil producers. Countries like Libya, Yemen, Algeria, and Saudi Arabia all need oil to be at over $100 a barrel to breakeven. Countries like Oman, Bahrain, Iran, the United Arab Emirates (UAE), and Iraq all need oil to be at over $50 to breakeven.[90]

In the age of cheap oil, buyers and sellers of oil may look for new, unconventional ways to buy/sell oil. Could one of these unconventional ways be AI systems that compete for oil sales?

AI is already managing oil prices, albeit for liters at the pump, not for barrels.

In Rotterdam, the Netherlands, two gas stations have deployed algorithms to undercut each other. They both use the same AI which mimics the moves of the other. When one gas station raises prices, by the end of the day the other gas station has done the same. But unlike in the past, when human gas store owners saw another gas station making changes and decided to follow suit, the algorithms are tapping huge pools of data and are given specific objectives, like increasing sales by a certain percentage.[91]

In the future, it could be countries, not gas stations using AI in this manner.

While Saudi Arabia needs oil to be at over $100 a barrel, Iran only needs oil to be over $50 a barrel. These two countries remain opposing powers in the Middle East, but any global oil crunch affects both nations the same way: they both depend on oil as their main source of revenue.

To compete in a new way, either country could launch an AI system to hurt the other.

For example, Iran, to hurt Saudi Arabia, could deploy an AI system that negotiates oil sales, changes Iran's oil prices in real time, and identifies new opportunities to sell oil. It might do all of this with the explicit, programmed objective of making sure oil never reaches more than $60 on purpose, to hurt Saudi Arabia which needs oil to be at over $100. Saudi Arabia on the other hand could deploy its own AI system and may want oil prices to rise above $100. But Saudi Arabia may not want Iran to supply oil. To accomplish this, Saudi Arabia's AI system may take extreme actions against Iran.

To hurt the other country, Iran and Saudi Arabia's AIs might not focus on fake news the way the e-commerce companies from China and the US might. Instead, the AI systems might focus on cyber attacks.

The AI systems would be acting autonomously, with pre-programmed objectives. Saudi Arabia's AI may be told that if Iran cuts oil prices by another 3%, it should launch cyber attacks at Iranian oil production facilities. It wouldn't be the first time Iran's oil production facilities have been hit by cyber attacks. In August 2016,

Iran directed its Supreme National Cyberspace Council to investigate a series of oil and petrochemical fires. Iran was worried that these fires were linked to a cyber attack and possibly to a virus, like Stuxnet.[92]

In the future, how would Iran respond if the cyber attack on oil production facilities was from Saudi Arabian AI? And that this AI was launching attacks because it had a pre-programmed agenda?

As AI systems deployed by Saudi Arabia and Iran compete with each other, they may change oil prices dozens or hundreds of times a day depending on how the AI systems are interpreting events and data. This will add a new level of volatility to global markets.

Alongside selling oil on world markets, AI systems may be used to forge new deals.

Increasingly, energy sales are revolving around two countries: China and India. While China has made huge strides in securing energy for itself, India has been slow to take action. With that said, in 2017, India's oil demand exceeded China's for the third year in a row.[93] As oil demand grows in India, several countries will be competing to become India's leading oil supplier.

In the future, India may launch an AI system to get the best oil deals. This AI system may be able to work with AI systems deployed by Saudi Arabia, Iran, and other oil exporters. These systems would communicate and piece together a proposal for an oil deal.

In February 2017, India announced that it will be launching two more strategic crude oil reserves to help protect the country from energy price volatility.[94] In the coming years, New Delhi may announce the creation of more such reserves. When this happens, Saudi Arabia and Iran's AI systems may be alerted that India wants to increase its strategic oil reserves. However, India's AI may make it clear that New Delhi will not pay more than $22 a barrel. With this, Saudi Arabia and Iran's AI systems would then approach India's AI. Now, AI systems from Iran, Saudi Arabia, and India, would be talking with each other and negotiating oil sales. Saudi Arabia's AI might propose oil for $21.89 a barrel, which India's AI would then let Iran know about. Iran's AI might respond with $21.86 a barrel and the cycle would repeat.

But other factors could also influence an oil deal negotiated by AI. Other nations may be alerted to India's oil strategy. And these nations might deploy their own AI systems to negotiate with India.

The US AI system could offer India oil for $21.43 a barrel. When Iran and Saudi Arabia learn of this, they may see the US as interfering in Middle Eastern oil affairs. The US may not care. It may want to lock in oil deals with India to grow its control over the oil market. This leads to a powerful possibility: could Iran and Saudi Arabia end up unintentionally working together to take on the US? In May 2018, reports emerged that Iran and Israel were in talks with each other in a hotel in Amman, Jordan. These were not direct talks. It was a Jordanian official that carried messages between the two parties.[95] In the same light, could Iran and Saudi Arabia start formulating a joint oil deal by having their AI systems work together? Instead of directly working together, they could use their AI systems as "middle-men". Or, going one step further, perhaps Jordan could deploy its own AI system to act as a "middle man" between the AI systems from Iran and Saudi Arabia.

An even more complex possibility exists here. Will Iran and Saudi Arabia know, at the beginning, that their AI systems are communicating with each other and exploring the possibility of a joint oil deal for India? If not, then when Iran and Saudi Arabia find out, they will be put in a challenging position. AI will have put them in a situation where they could work together. Iran and Saudi Arabia will have two options: agree with what their AI systems are doing or restrain their AI systems from doing so.

In other words, AI could create new ways in which nations interact with each other. And this may influence certain relationships, like that of Iran and Saudi Arabia.

To Protect Local Companies, AI Cartels May Exist

Governments could also tap AI to protect their economy and local businesses.

After the 2016 presidential elections in the US, the new administration vowed to "level the playing field" for US businesses, both at home and abroad. It specifically called for the removal of high taxes and tariffs applied to US goods that are exported abroad.

To deal with unfair trade, the US could turn to AI competition.

Today, AI systems compete with each other in various industries. However, most of the time this competition has to do with raising prices. [96] Could AI systems work together to reduce prices? And could these

AI systems have political or economic objectives?

In the future, the US government may launch a scheme to help its automakers compete with foreign cars in the US market. Part of this scheme may be an "AI cartel" made up of US car companies. The AI cartel would be an AI system that communicates with US car companies in real time to sell US cars.

The AI system will not just be working to sell US cars, but also to "corner the market".

Tomorrow, as people purchase vehicles online, platforms may use AI to find people the best deals. If a person searches for a car for $26,000, a Japanese car dealership might offer a vehicle for $25,000. But the American AI system might immediately work with local US dealerships and price a US vehicle for $23,000. In fact, the US government might offer dealerships a subsidy for whatever they lose. For example, if AI sells a US vehicle for $23,000 but the dealership takes a hit of $1,000, the US government may reimburse the dealership for $1,000. The goal is to give US car companies the security that the government has their back and that they should beat foreign car companies no matter the cost.

As the AI cartel in the US results in foreign car companies losing huge amounts of business, foreign governments could be irked. Because the US government supports its AI cartel, foreign governments may have to take matters into their own hands.

This could force countries to create their own AI cartels. In Japan, AI cartels might work to ensure US financial companies cannot sell their services. When a US investment bank tries to sell financial services to a pension group in Japan, the AI cartel in Japan may work with Japanese investment banks to procure a counter offer. Then the Japanese AI cartel may approach the pension group in Japan to beat the US.

Once again, AI competition could draw new geopolitical lines in the world and create conflicts between governments.

Conclusion

For countries, when discussing what future economic competition will look like, the main ideas all revolve around re-negotiating trade deals, adopting new currencies, or changing the role that government plays. However, these ideas are not new. They have been practiced for decades.

As the global economy changes, competition between nations and companies is going to rise to levels never seen before. This will force capitals and boardrooms to look for new tools to rise above the noise, one of which may be using AI. As AI helps countries and companies compete, it will mean competition is no longer driven by people, but by technology.

In the past, whenever a country or company made a new decision, the world could look back on history for a precedent. But there is no precedent to fall back on with AI competition. And that means AI competition could become a new geopolitical quagmire for countries.

Nations that try to regulate AI competition will end up, explicitly or implicitly, favoring one country over another. Nations that ignore AI competition will see AI from various businesses roam free, potentially hurting consumers and the business environment.

Perhaps the single biggest area of uncertainty is what competition will look like when AI takes over. For decades, if not centuries, disruption has come in the form of economic recession or breakdown of government. These events do not take place often and the gaps between them allow for a more stable global economy to operate.

When it comes to AI though, all stability gets thrown out of the window. Disruption that may have come every five or ten years could emerge every week or month as AI makes decisions that nobody expected or thought of.

In other words, the way in which the global economy is analyzed will need to change as AI drives trade, economic decisions, and more.

The future of relations between countries might not depend on how experienced a government's diplomatic team is or how long the countries have been allies, but on the very decisions AI is making to compete and win.

Chapter 6
AI Workers

Brasilia, Brazil
2033

As the president of Brazil eats her dinner, her smartphone vibrates with an alert. The alert is part of a new system the government has deployed, which provides real-time updates and daily reports on the state of the economy. The alerts go to the president, her advisors, and her cabinet.

As the president reads the latest report, her fork drops. According to the report, in the last 24 hours, over 250,000 workers have disappeared in Brazil. The economy has come to a grinding halt.

As she reads the report, a group of senior advisors rush into the room with red faces. They have known about the 250,000 workers disappearing but had postponed telling the president until they knew everything.

According to the president's advisors, 250,000 workers did disappear in the last 24 hours. Except they were not human workers but AI workers. Because these workers have disappeared, tens thousands of businesses in Brazil are crippled.

Neither the president nor her advisors have any idea as to why this has happened or what to do. While discussing possibilities, the minister of foreign affairs enters the room and requests the president's attention. Standing in a corner, the foreign minister explains that he was sent an anonymous message. The message stated that the AI workers disappeared as retaliation for a deal Brazil recently signed with China. The deal made China the sole supplier of AI to certain sectors in Brazil, like transportation, finance, and healthcare.

Through this deal, China has a monopoly over AI in Brazil.

A few seconds pass until the president responds.

"Are you telling me that, because of our decision regarding Chinese AI, someone has shut down our AI workers?".

"It sure looks that way", the foreign minister replies.

"Who could do such a thing?", the president inquires anxiously.

"Well... there is only one country whose AI we have relied on for so long", the foreign minister says. "The United States".

Introduction

Workers have had a huge impact on the way nations develop and move forward. But never has the workforce of a country been viewed as geopolitical. This is because the human workforce of a country has been local not foreign. What does this mean?

Canada has more than 18 million workers for a population of more than 36 million.[97] These workers live in Canada, as citizens, permanent residents, or new immigrants. They are working to build a life for themselves. Canada does not have to worry about these workers leaving the country en masse or disappearing. But what if a small but significant portion of Canada's workforce were foreign AI workers?

Then Canadian businesses may have been dependent on AI workers and Canada might have been worried. Part of Canada's workforce would no longer be local; it would be foreign and unfamiliar.

The AI workers would work for Canadian companies and abide by Canadian laws. But they may be supplied by another country. This is a huge geopolitical risk. Tomorrow, if Canada clashes with the country that supplies the AI workers, these workers might stop working or simply disappear. How would Canada deal with 25% or 45% of its AI workers disappearing at the "flick of a switch"?

Countries supplying workers is not a new concept - except it has always revolved around living, breathing people.

For years in Africa, China has brought its own workers to different infrastructure projects. In Angola, a resource-rich country in southern Africa, more than 200,000 Chinese workers are present - the second highest number of Chinese workers in Africa.[98] There are fifty state-owned Chinese firms and four hundred private Chinese companies operating in Angola. [99] The problem is, Chinese firms only hire Chinese workers for projects and not locals. In Angola, Chinese firms are even ignoring a law which requires 30% of labor to go to Angolans. When Angolans do get jobs, they are entry level.

For Angola, is this a fair relationship with China, its largest trading partner? Not exactly.

But for China, it is a powerful strategy. China controls the labor force that Angola's economy relies on. This is a huge vulnerability for Angola. Should relations between China and Angola deteriorate, China might call its workers back home. Chinese labor would disappear and the Angolan economy might break down as infrastructure projects come to a halt.

This same risk emerges, and exponentially increases, with AI.

As economies become dependent on AI, governments need to begin asking where the AI is coming from. AI systems, whether in banking, transportation, healthcare, education or policing, are the next workers. And the more a nation depends on AI workers from a foreign country, the more power that foreign country could have.

US Turns Off China's Healthcare System Through AI

The main way countries will depend on AI workers is through automation. And in the coming years, automation could make up a large percentage of a country's workforce as it eats up jobs.

In November 2017, researchers published a study projecting that automation would take 800 million jobs by 2030.[100] In January 2016, a university in the United Kingdom published a report showing the risk automation poses to specific countries. Ethiopia had the highest risk, with 85% of jobs at risk of being automated. That number dropped to 77% in China and 69% in India. [101] The job displacement from automation is not too far. It is already happening. In January 2017, a Japanese life insurance company replaced 34 workers with an AI service from the US.[102]

As companies depend on AI workers, supplied by other countries, a new geopolitical risk could emerge. Could AI workers be shut down if geopolitical tensions rise in the future?

One of the world's most successful AI services comes from a US technology services company. And one country where this AI service has entered is China. In August 2016, the US firm partnered with an organization in China that uses AI to fight cancer. The partnership will see American AI deployed in 21 Chinese hospitals to help provide new cancer treatment options.[103] In June 2017, the US firm also partnered with a Chinese health services firm to take the US's AI throughout China.[104]

As the US technology services firm strikes these deals, it comes at a time when China is looking to AI to manage its healthcare system. As China does this, potentially hundreds of millions of people in China could become dependent on AI doctors supplied by the US. Does China realize what is taking place? China is slowly becoming dependent on US AI workers.

The US may be able to exploit this dependency if tensions flare with China in the future.

One possible strain between the US and China relationship is Taiwan. In June 2018, the US opened a brand new complex in Taiwan to house its embassy.[105] This upset Beijing, which has been trying to ensure the world never sees Taiwan as independent from China. A few months earlier, in March 2018, after the US announced plans to strengthen ties with Taiwan, a Chinese state-run newspaper said that China should prepare military action against Taiwan.[106]

In the coming years, tensions could again skyrocket between the US and China over Taiwan.

At this point, the US may have a new way to respond to China.

In the past, when the US did something that aggravated China, one of the ways China responded was by targeting US firms. For example, in May 2014 (following the global outburst over US surveillance), China ordered its state-run firms to stop employing US consulting firms. China was worried that these consulting firms were spying for Washington.[107]

Similarly, if China does something that provokes the US, the US could respond in kind. But instead of banning Chinese firms in the US, could the US ban its own firms in China?

This may seem illogical. Why would the US want to stop its firms from operating in China? Because, unlike in the past when US firms were simply growing their businesses, US firms in the future may be also supplying AI workers. By pulling these firms from China, these workers would disappear, creating chaos in China.

If the US temporarily bans the US technology services company from supplying AI doctors to China, it could pull the rug from under China's healthcare system.

The US AI doctors would disappear. What will people in China do if they cannot diagnose a problem, access a medical treatment, or ask important questions? The US AI doctors may also be linked to local hospitals and pharmacies, which use the AI to fill prescriptions in real time. How will China respond to the US sabotaging its healthcare system through AI?

China may decide to respond in kind.

If the US targets China's healthcare system, China might target the US manufacturing sector.

Just as China's healthcare system may be dependent on American AI, the US manufacturing sector could be dependent on Chinese AI. In December 2016, a Chinese appliance maker bought a leading German robotics firm.[108] One of the stated goals is to make the German robotics firm the number one robotics supplier in China. [109] Tomorrow, the German robotics firm may want to become the biggest supplier in the US as well.

In the future, tens of thousands of German robots, owned by a Chinese company, might be working in factories across the US. This may greatly improve productivity and output but it would mean the US is dependent on Chinese robot workers.

If the US pulls AI workers from China, then China might pull robot workers from the US. The Chinese might turn off all the German robots in the US. Perhaps China has a backdoor into these robots' operating system. If China pulls robot workers from the US and crashes parts of the US manufacturing sector, could it start the next recession in parts of the US economy?

If so, China would be hurting the US economy - not through selling US debt or ditching the US dollar, but by turning off robot workers.

Hacking AI Workers Is A New Possibility

Another risk that comes with AI workers is hacking. It is impossible to hack a human worker today (unless they are transhumanists). But AI workers, being technology, could be hacked and used to damage a country.

Already, many popular robots have weak defenses against hacking.

In March 2017, a cyber security consulting firm published a report on robots from various robotics companies. The consulting firm found that these robots are susceptible to being hacked. Some functions of these robots could be controlled even if the user does not have proper authentication.[110] In May 2017, researchers from Italy and Japan, hacked a robot arm from a Swedish robotics company. The operating system (OS) of the arm costs $75,000. The researchers were able to hijack it with a USB. Once inside, the researchers were able to control the machine. One way the researchers hijacked the robot was by making it draw an uneven line when it was tasked with drawing a straight line. The line was not perceptibly uneven; it was uneven at the micro-scale. This is extremely dangerous as many robot arms are deployed in aerospace and other industries where precision is paramount. Even the slightest inaccuracy in a straight line could cause the final product to fail or crash.[111]

Like the robot arm, could future AI workers be hacked to cause damage?

In 2015, the South Korean government directed a South Korean technology company to develop robots to replace Chinese labor.[112] At the same time, South Korea has the highest robot density in the world with 631 robots for every 10,000 workers.[113] This means that South Korea's economy is becoming increasingly "robot dependent". And this could make South Korea vulnerable to hacking.

One way to hack robots is to make them break down and shut off. Another way is to make them purposefully manufacture products with built-in defects, such as a faulty circuit board, screen, or battery.

In 2016, popular South Korean smartphones were reported to be "exploding".[114] After an investigation, the manufacturer of the smartphones said the problem was the way the batteries were manufactured. Specifically, there wasn't enough space between a "protective casing" around the battery and the battery components themselves.[115]

But what if the manufacturer found that its robots had been hacked and were purposefully making the batteries the wrong way? Should the investigation find that the hackers originated from China or North Korea, South Korea would face a new kind of geopolitical challenge.

From South Korea's standpoint, it has not just been hacked. Its economy has been threatened and its businesses sabotaged. And the way this was done was not through vulnerable routers in a government network but through tens of thousands of robots that South Korea had deployed in factories.

With South Korea's robot workers sabotaged, South Korean companies may have to stop production of certain components or South Korean companies may need to engage in massive recalls costing tens of billions of dollars.

However, what happens if it was a partner that hacked into South Korean factories, such as Japan? Perhaps Japan did it to slow down South Korean firms and give its own companies a boost.

This leads to a new possibility.

In the past, nations used subsidies or intellectual property law to limit how foreign companies operated and grew. In the future, nations might hack robot and AI workers to achieve the same goal.

Conclusion

As automation eats up jobs, governments and societies will panic. But among the challenges of social unrest, basic income, and job creation, is another challenge: where are these AI systems coming from?

Unless countries develop their own AI ecosystems, most of the world will be importing AI from abroad. In other words, governments could be "importing" the automation of jobs. These AI systems represent the new workforce of companies and nations.

Certain governments may ignore this risk. After all, today countries import microwaves, cars, televisions, dish washers, air conditioners, ovens, refrigerators, lawn mowers, and barbecues from abroad. All these items have technology built into them and none of these items pose a real risk to a country's national security or economy. The important point here is that none of those items are acting as labor.

When a nation has one hundred thousand, five hundred thousand or even one million AI workers, it will create a new risk. When countries are dependent on AI workers, it means their economy and businesses may be dependent on a foreign workforce supplied by another country.

To protect the economy, certain governments might introduce public policy around AI.

Governments might require AI companies to undergo additional screening before they can sell AI. Perhaps foreign AI firms will be forced to hand over all control of their AI to a local authority or organization.

What is more likely is that countries will be left in a vacuum of uncertainty.

For the first time in history, workers are no longer locally based and permanent. They could be foreign, digital, and could disappear at a moment's notice.

This makes AI the most perplexing technology to ever emerge.

On one hand, AI will create tremendous benefits for economies and societies.

But on the other hand, AI will be creating tremendous risks and vulnerabilities for economies and societies.

In other words, the more AI "works", the more vulnerable a country may become.

Chapter 7
AI Bias

Tokyo, Japan
2031

In 2031, Japan launches a new AI initiative.

Going forward, AI will be in charge of managing and delivering all government services. Unless humans are explicitly required, AI will take over everything from emergency services to collecting taxes to public transportation.

As people in Japan use this new system, it is met with great applause.

Bureaucracy is cut in half. Corruption and graft decline. Citizen satisfaction surges. And, other countries, like France and the United Arab Emirates (UAE), approach Japan to buy the AI system.

But one country becomes increasingly frustrated with Japan's new system: Australia.

Part of what Japan's AI manages is patents. AI decides who can register a patent and what the terms and conditions will be. Before the AI system, 45% of patents that Australian businesses filed were approved. Now, just 10% are being approved. Australian businesses, worried that their inventions and innovations are vulnerable in Japan, call on the Australian government to take action.

Australia questions Japan about its new AI system. Why are more Australian businesses being rejected after the AI system was introduced? Australia demands an explanation. Japan refuses to concede.

Angry, the Australian government vows to retaliate. At the same time, other countries, like India and China, notice that their patent requests are being approved more than in the past.

Deep down, Japan's political leadership is well aware of what is going on.

When the AI was created, it was programmed with a bias. The bias is against what Japan views as the "old world" and is designed to help Japan align with the "new world" by favoring patent applications from new and emerging economic powers. This is why Australian businesses are being rejected while Indian and Chinese businesses are being approved.

Through AI, Japan is trying to change its geopolitical alignment.

And so far, it appears to be working.

Introduction

As AI is deployed around the world, one of the biggest concerns is whether AI systems will have a bias. AI could hold certain prejudices or stereotypes about people because of their skin color, religion, gender, ethnicity, or culture. AI could exclude certain people because of stereotypes or prejudices it has learned, absorbed, or even been taught. This bias has the potential to affect the overall behavior and the decisions an AI system makes.

Examples of AI bias have already been observed when AI has been deployed in certain settings.

In March 2016, a US technology firm launched an AI chatbot on social media. The project started off smoothly but in the span of 24 hours, the chatbot had become racist and misogynistic. Less than a day after the chatbot was launched, the technology firm took it down. [116] Separately, in September 2016, an AI system was appointed the judge of an international beauty contest. It was up to the AI to decide which men and women would be selected as the winners. More than 6,000 people from around the world submitted pictures. Yet, the winners the AI selected were almost entirely Caucasian. This led to questions of whether the AI had a bias, causing it to rule out people who were not Caucasian.[117]

Why did both the chatbot and AI judge exhibit these biases? Because they were learning from people to become smarter. In April 2017, a team of researchers at a university in the United Kingdom published a study about how AI becomes biased. They found that as AI crunches huge amounts of data, it absorbs the biases, stereotypes, and prejudices within this data. This causes AI to have gender and ethnic biases.[118]

While bias may already exist in certain technologies, what makes AI bias fundamentally different is the scale at which AI will be handling tasks. Because this scale will be infinitely larger than what humans handle today, AI bias could be extremely dangerous.

Until now, AI bias has revolved around skin color, gender, or religion. But there is another kind of AI bias that could emerge in the future: political bias. AI could soon become biased because of the political situation between countries or by simply operating in a certain region of the world. AI could treat people or businesses unfairly because of what is taking place in the world of geopolitics.

Navigating A Biased Court System, Managed By AI

In November 2016, the head of China's Supreme People's Court, the highest court in China, spoke at a conference. He said that future courts will be smarter by taking advantage of AI, along with big data and cloud computing. One of the objectives of China's court system is to "teach" AI to learn from previous rulings.[119] At the time of these comments, 178 courts in Hebei province (northern China) had already deployed AI, helping close to 3,000 judges handle 150,000 cases. As AI helps judges in China, it may be used to decide whether someone is guilty. In November 2016, a study was published by two researchers from a university in China. The researchers claimed to have tested AI that can tell if someone is a convicted criminal just by looking at their "facial features".[120]

These developments point to China's future court systems being managed by AI.

As AI manages China's court systems, it may begin ruling (or advise a ruling) against people for geopolitical reasons. The AI may have a political bias. AI with political bias could create new geopolitical tensions between countries.

In November 2017, a Taiwanese activist who went missing in China was sentenced to five years in a Chinese prison for "suspicion of subversion" (challenging the Chinese government's power).[121] A year before the arrest of the activist, in April 2016, Kenya deported Taiwanese nationals to China, an act which Taiwan called kidnapping.[122] These nationals were charged with cyber crimes.

Today, Taiwan blames China for these arrests. But in the future, when AI is in charge, will Taiwan blame China's AI?

The way Taiwanese nationals are treated in China's court system could be very different when AI is in charge. Chinese AI may take into account the relationship between China and Taiwan. The AI might know that, for decades, China has viewed Taiwan as part of China but Taiwan has viewed itself as an independent country. The AI might also know that China has long tried to maintain a grip over Taiwan's foreign policy but Taiwan has become harder and harder to control. Because of this viewpoint, the AI may rule against Taiwanese nationals with increased severity, as a way to "punish" Taiwan. These sentences may deviate from previous rulings for similar crimes.

How will Taiwan react if its citizens are being jailed or punished in China with harsher than normal sentences, while Chinese locals or people from other nationalities, are receiving less severe sentences for the same crimes?

Taipei may see China's AI as biased because of geopolitics.

If Taiwan notices that as it tries to be more independent, China's AI hands out more severe sentences to its nationals, Taiwan will be forced to operate in a new era of geopolitics. For the first time, China will be dealing with Taiwan through AI. And Taiwan will have to respond in some way.

In August 2017, Taiwan announced that it will be investing USD $527 million into AI over the next four to five years. The plan calls for the creation of AI research centers along with AI manufacturing and development hubs.[123] In the coming years, Taiwan may decide to expand its AI focus to include law and order. Taiwan might put AI in charge of its court systems.

At this point in time, Taiwan will have to make a geopolitical decision. Will it purposefully program its AI to be biased against China? Or, will Taiwan allow its AI to learn on its own and make objective judgments?

This question is part of an ongoing conversation within the AI world about how AI will become biased. For now, there are two ways that bias can emerge. First, AI can learn a bias based on the data it has access to. China's AI, for example, could be biased because it has been absorbing skewed data.

Second, AI can have a bias because someone programs the bias into the AI.

Taiwan, seeking to retaliate against China, may program a bias into its AI. Now, Chinese nationals arrested in Taiwan, either for serious crimes such as murder or theft, or less serious crimes like public intoxication or littering, could be subject to a biased AI. These nationals could receive highly "irregular" sentences. China, watching this take place, may program more bias into its AI court systems, creating a "tit for tat" situation between China and Taiwan.

The same AI used within China or Taiwan's court system, may also be used in policing or the delivery of government services. That means that bias could extend to other areas, affecting either country even more.

Also consider that this may not be limited to China and Taiwan.

Like in the past, when governments watched conflicts and learned from them, AI may also be watching and learning. If Vietnam also has an AI court system, its AI may be watching how AI court systems are behaving in China and Taiwan. Vietnam's AI may believe that Chinese and Taiwanese nationals deserve a more severe sentence because that is what has happened in the past. Now, Vietnamese AI may hold a bias towards Chinese and Taiwanese nationals. This could cause friction between Vietnam, China, and Taiwan.

AI bias is not just a country-specific risk. It has regional, if not global ramifications.

When AI Decides Whether You Can Enter A Country

Alongside the court system is border security. And slowly AI is taking over this area as well.

In February 2018, the Ministry of Interior in the United Arab Emirates (UAE) unveiled a plan to use AI in national security. Part of this plan calls for the automation of border security officers. The UAE wants to replace border security officers with AI by 2020.[124] In the future, people who get off the plane at Dubai or Abu Dhabi, may simply walk into the UAE.

Once again, political bias may play a role here.

In August 2017, an Iranian man was sentenced to 10 years in prison for allegedly spying on the UAE and attempting to hurt UAE-US relations.[125] This was not the first time arrests were made over Iranian spying. In 2013, a Pakistani national was accused of spying for Iran.[126]

As AI decides who enters the UAE, will it treat everyone equally or will certain people from certain countries be stopped more than often?

After the UAE automates its border security in 2020, there may be a 40% increase in the number of Iranian nationals detained and arrested. Iran may see this as a bias. As AI manages immigration in the UAE, Iran may question why Iranians are being arrested more than normal.

Iran will be forced to take steps if its citizens are facing a biased AI system in the UAE.

Whatever steps Iran takes, from telling its citizens and businesses to stop investing in the UAE to turning back Emirati goods at the border, Tehran will see its relationship deteriorate with the UAE because of AI.

But there is also another way Iran can respond. Iran is part of a new, emerging group of powers, alongside China, Russia, and India. In April 2018, Iran joined the Eurasian Economic Union (EEU), an economic union led by Russia and made up of countries in Eastern Europe and Central Asia.[127] It is possible that in the future, the EEU may have a unified AI system, helping manage trade, immigration, and border security. This means that if the UAE's AI has a bias towards Iran, the EEU's AI may have a bias towards the UAE.

Inputting bias into AI could be the new way countries get back at each other.

Having Trouble Registering A Patent? Blame AI Bias

It is not just courts and borders that could experience AI bias. AI is slowly making its way into government services as well, such as patent registration. This means patent registration could soon have an AI bias.

In April 2017, Japan's Patent Office announced that it will begin using AI to process patents. By 2018, Japan wants this AI to be able to conduct up to 20 different tasks, including search requests and being able to check, through image recognition, if a technology has already been patented.[128]

Patents have always been a way to see how advanced a nation is. The more patents a country has, the more power they have. In the future, the most important patents are likely to be those in AI and robotics. Japan is already a leader here. A Japanese car company has the most patents for technology related to self-driving cars and Japanese firms hold the first, second, and third places for robotics patents.[129] At the same time, Japan has the second most AI patents in the world (after the US).[130]

As Japan looks to keep its edge with AI patents, businesses from other countries may want to register patents to protect their innovations. One country they may want to register patents in is Japan.

If businesses from China apply for patents in Japan, will they face pushback from Japan's AI?

In the future, Japan's AI may be given more control over patent registration. For example, the AI may be able to approve a patent for further review. Japan's AI, however, may have a bias towards China. It may be learning about the growth of China's economy and businesses. To help Japan compete, the AI might reject patent requests from Chinese businesses.

How will Chinese businesses react to their patent requests being rejected by AI?

The Chinese government may step in and claim there is a political element to how Japan's AI is behaving. This could be the case if Japan's AI is rejecting patents from Chinese firms, but approving similar or the same patent requests from Indian or Mexican firms.

How will China respond? Perhaps by targeting Japan's robotics industry.

China is the world's largest market for industrial robots. And Japan has the world's largest maker of industrial robots. However, this company is becoming dependent on China. In April 2017, it announced that in response to rising demand in China, it was building a $566 million plant in Ibaraki Prefecture, northeast of Tokyo, to build more robots.[131]

As China becomes the most important market for Japan's robotics companies, it could also become a huge vulnerability for Japan. Should Japanese AI reject Chinese patent requests, China could respond by banning its factories from buying Japanese robots. How will Japan deal with this blow? Japan's economy could be threatened and its industrial robot firms could be put at risk.

This shows that AI bias means as much for businesses as it does for governments.

Conclusion

Bias has long been a fear of people. Whether in business or government, systems have been designed to have as little bias as possible. The reality though is that no matter how far organizations go, bias will always exist. This bias will not disappear in the age of AI. If anything, it could reach new heights.

Alongside judging people based on physical or cultural attributes, like their skin color, gender, or religion, AI may begin to judge people and form biases based on where a person is coming from and what the geopolitical situation is with that country. And considering that AI may be in control of trade, foreign policy, court systems and more, the decisions AI makes could have huge ramifications for people and businesses.

Calls to program AI in a way that reduces bias should not go unheard, but they should not be viewed as the final solution either. Pushes to create AI rules, including around AI bias, will require countries to agree on exactly what rules to adopt. Should AI adopt Christian, Jewish, or Muslim rules? What about Hindu or Buddhist beliefs? When it comes to history, should the AI be looking at the world through the filters of North America, Asia, Europe, or Africa?

Each of these questions carries its own consequences. And each of these decisions is geopolitical. This means that AI bias is inevitable because AI will be developed and programmed differently, based on where it is coming from.

If AI bias is inevitable, then the geopolitical challenges that will stem from it are not a question of whether, but a question of when.

The biggest risk when it comes to AI bias is how far up the chain the bias goes.

If AI is in charge of how nations communicate or is acting as a foreign policy advisor, then bias may exist at multiple levels. This means AI bias could have an even greater effect on the outcome of disputes and challenges.

AI bias may be intentional or unintentional. It may emerge from the US or China. And it may be present in foreign policy or trade. But regardless of how and where AI bias comes from, nations will begin to see it as a tool that they can use to limit what another country can do. And if this becomes the norm, then AI bias could have a bigger impact on the world than any other kind of bias can ever have.

Chapter 8
AI Policing

Seoul, South Korea
2029

In 2028, China rolls out a new predictive policing system to reduce crime.

The new system has a dual use. It tracks locals and it tracks foreigners. For the first time, people visiting China could be arrested based on predictions that China's system makes.

Shortly after China rolls out this system, China and South Korea get embroiled in a new dispute over a deal between South Korea and India. Under the deal, Seoul will deploy an Indian missile defense system on its border, powered entirely by AI.

China demands that South Korea pull out from this deal as it puts China's national security at risk.

Seoul ignores this.

As tensions rise, a separate challenge emerges. There is a spike in the number of South Koreans being detained in China over predictions China's predictive policing system is making. Increasingly, South Koreans are being fined or arrested for petty crimes. South Korea demands that China look into the situation.

Beijing ignores this.

In 2029, China's predictive policing system goes beyond detaining average South Koreans. It arrests a delegation of South Korean business executives, representing South Korean multinationals. They are arrested over drug and prostitution predictions. And they are sentenced in Chinese courts and receive jail time.

Relations between China and South Korea take a nosedive. Seoul bans its citizens from traveling to China and South Korean businesses panic over their operations in China. As China and South Korea issue threats to each other, South Korea directs its intelligence agency, the Korean Central Intelligence Agency (KCIA), to take action.

The KCIA hacks into the predictive policing system of Japan and Taiwan and messes with the code. Now, Chinese nationals in Japan and Taiwan are being targeted more than people from other countries.

Tensions soar in Asia.

Policing has never been a variable of geopolitics. Thanks to AI, now it is.

Introduction

Since its inception, policing has followed the same model. A government enforces a law. People break the law or begin the process of breaking the law. Then police arrest these people (or try to).

Thanks to AI, a different model is now emerging. This new model is called "predictive policing" and it will allow police around the world to predict a crime before the crime takes place. This includes predicting the person carrying out the crime.

For years, predictive policing has been popularized by Hollywood movies. But when these movies came out, the technology behind predictive policing did not exist. Now it does.

In 2018, the Los Angeles Police Department (LAPD) was reported to be using predictive policing technology, supplied by a US technology firm, to identify "probable offenders".[132] A few years earlier, in 2015, a university in the US held a predictive policing pilot with the LAPD. The university supplied an algorithm to help the LAPD decide where it should place officers. Using the algorithm, the LAPD saw crime drop two-fold. [133] By 2019, South Korea wants to have a predictive policing system called "Crime Layout Understanding Engine" (CLUE) up and running. CLUE will be a massive database that stores information and allows police to search and share things. At the same time, CLUE will analyze variables like real estate prices and weather conditions to predict future crime. [134] For the 2020 Tokyo Olympics, police in Japan are working on a system that can identify whether a single person is responsible for multiple crimes and predict what kind of crime this person will commit next.[135]

From the US to South Korea to Japan, a new era of policing is on the horizon. Until now, policing, whether by people or AI, has been largely "localized". This means that usually governments deploy policing systems to protect or arrest locals. But in the era of AI, this may change. AI could predict that a foreigner will commit a crime. Or governments may deploy predictive policing systems in other countries. Predictive policing does not just point to a new era of policing. It also points to a convergence between policing and geopolitics, two domains that have remained separate until now.

Predictive Policing Could Fuel North Korea-South Korea Tensions

In April 2018, a major geopolitical reset took place. The leaders of North Korea and South Korea met at the Demilitarized Zone (DMZ).[136] It was the first time a North Korean leader had crossed the DMZ into South Korea since 1953. A few months later, in June, the US president and the leader of North Korea met. It was the surest sign yet of peace on the Korean Peninsula. But these meetings weren't just symbolic. They were intended to convince North Korea of the enormous economic potential peace can bring. When the leaders of North Korea and South Korea met, South Korea's leader handed his North Korean counterpart a USB. On it was maps, charts, and other data, showing how the two Koreas could connect economically and how North Korea could rapidly industrialize.[137]

Lasting peace between North Korea and South Korea is likely to fall on reconnecting North Korea back into the global economy. Yet, even as this happens, there will always be the chance that tensions resurface. Future tensions however, may not be over missile launches or the deployment of soldiers. They could surface over other issues, like trade.

In the coming years, as trade between the two Koreas picks up, Pyongyang might complain that Seoul is taxing North Korean goods too high or that South Korean companies are dumping products in the

North. After all, South Korea's economy is much larger and South Korean businesses have far more resources and experience. If South Korea does not adjust its trade policies, tensions between North Korea and South Korea could rise.

Could North Korea retaliate through predictive policing?

As North Korea industrializes, it may make use of AI to develop. What does using AI to develop mean?

In Ethiopia, entrepreneurs are calling on the government to invest in AI to transform the country. Instead of following a traditional development model, such as farm to factory, factory to office, Ethiopia's entrepreneurs want to follow a model that gives people the skills to take advantage of AI and other new technologies.[138]

One way North Korea could develop through AI (and strengthen government control over society) is by deploying a predictive policing system. Instead of investing in the newest policing tactics or building giant police forces, North Korea could invest in AI and skip the traditional model.

North Korea could use its predictive policing system to strike back at South Korea over trade issues. For example, Pyongyang could direct its system to target South

Korean nationals. As more South Koreans travel to North Korea, a handful of them may be arrested over "future crimes".

Seoul may raise the issue with the North Korean government. North Korea could deny that its predictive policing system is acting abnormally or that it has a bias towards South Koreans. Instead, North Korea could justify the actions of its system, saying that the South Korean nationals arrested had a high risk of breaking North Korean law.

Initially, South Korea may not take action. But what happens if North Korea's system goes beyond targeting average South Koreans and starts to identify and arrest more important people, like an executive from a major South Korean multinational over drug predictions or a South Korean athlete over prostitution predictions?

Over time, South Korea may see a pattern. As trade tensions grow, more South Korean nationals may be arrested in North Korea over future crimes.

Eventually, South Korea may respond in an equally unconventional way. South Korea might turn to its allies, such as the US and Japan, and have them direct their own predictive policing systems to arrest North Korean nationals.

This would raise a new challenge.

South Korea, the US, and Japan may "mold" their predictive policing systems to target the same people. Or, South Korea might just hack these systems. In fact, the next phase of government intrusion might revolve around hacking into advanced AI systems that govern societies, including predictive policing systems and adjusting their behavior.

How would North Korea react if its nationals are being arrested, in unusually high numbers in the US and Japan, due to predictive policing? Pyongyang might see this as "tit for tat". North Korea, seeing its nationals arrested in the US and Japan, could turn to its allies, such as China and Russia. North Korea could ask them to adjust their predictive policing systems to target people from the US and Japan. Then US and Japanese nationals could be at a higher risk of being arrested in China and Russia over future crimes. What was initially a problem between South Korea and North Korea would now involve several countries. For the first time, the way AI polices a society could have consequences hundreds or thousands of miles away.

At the same time, what if predictive policing systems learn and adjust their behavior autonomously? In the future, a handful of metropolises in India may have predictive policing systems. To prepare for future crimes, these systems may be watching what is going on in the world, including what other predictive policing systems are doing.

Based on that, India's systems may update themselves. Could India's systems automatically target North Korean nationals because of what takes place between North Korea and South Korea? India's systems may view South Korea as more "important" to New Delhi than North Korea. India's systems may see any "attack" on South Korean nationals as "bad" or "wrong". Because of this "bias", India's systems may automatically target North Korean nationals, even though North Korea has caused no harm to India directly.

Understanding The Trade Around Predictive Policing

Another important part of predictive policing is the trade of these systems.

In 2014, Chinese police began patrolling tourist areas in Paris, alongside French police. The goal was to ensure that Chinese tourists, who are becoming a huge part of French tourism, are safe from theft and other crimes. [139] Since then, Chinese police have also been deployed in several other countries, including Italy [140] and Zambia.[141]

In other words, countries are "importing" police from China.

In the case of North Korea, where would it get a predictive policing system from?

It is possible that North Korea could develop its own system. In May 2018, a think tank published a report on how North Korea has been marketing certain technologies. This included vehicle recognition software in Turkey, fingerprint scanning technology in Nigeria, encryption technology in Malaysia, and even facial recognition technologies for law enforcement. [142] If North Korea can develop these kinds of technologies in isolation, once North Korea is "plugged back" into the world, it could develop more advanced technologies.

However, it is more likely that North Korea would purchase a predictive policing system from abroad, such as from China. It may be faster for North Korea to do this. If this happens, it would mean that Chinese AI is policing North Korean society. A version of this has already happened in Malaysia. In February 2018, a Chinese startup began supplying a division of Malaysia's police force with facial recognition cameras. [143]

Malaysian police are now using Chinese AI to catch criminals.

As predictive policing systems are sold, it could give foreign countries control over how a society functions.

For example, China might export its predictive policing system to Venezuela. But China may keep a back door in this system. Shortly after deploying the system in Venezuela, China and Japan may find themselves in a geopolitical conflict. As this conflict grows, China could use its back door in Venezuela. China could direct the predictive policing system to target people from Japan. Now, as people from Japan travel to Venezuela, they may be arrested while on public transportation, questioned at clubs and bars, or even detained the moment they land. Venezuela may not even know that China has meddled with its predictive policing system. How would Japan deal with this kind of attack on its people through AI? How will Venezuela react if it finds out that China has meddled with its predictive policing system?

Consider that Venezuela may be one of dozens of countries where China's predictive policing system may be in use. This creates a new geopolitical reality for the world: any country that picks a fight with

China will have to deal with China's global AI capabilities and reach.

Selling predictive policing systems could also be a new way to support groups.

Tomorrow, if there is turmoil in Tunisia that divides the country up into several warring factions, Russia could step in and supply one of the factions with advanced, predictive policing technology. Because of this technology, the Russian-backed faction could have more control over Tunisian society, potentially allowing it to succeed in unifying the country. Once this faction succeeds, it may have stronger ties with Russia than anyone else.

In the future, instead of sending arms or money, countries may send predictive policing systems to support a certain group or government.

Using Predictive Policing To Warn Citizens Before They Are Arrested

Predictive policing is usually looked at from the viewpoint of the country deploying it, such as North Korea or China. But, if one country is using predictive policing to arrest people, another country may use predictive policing to stop its people from being arrested.

In March 2016, a former Indian naval officer was arrested in Balochistan, one of the four provinces of Pakistan. Intelligence agencies in Pakistan believed that he was an agent of the Research & Analysis Wing (RAW), the foreign intelligence agency of India. In April 2017, more than a year after his arrest, the alleged spy was sentenced to death. [144] India asserted that the person arrested was not a spy and that he was kidnapped in Iran, not arrested in Pakistan. Regardless of whether this person was an Indian spy or not, the capture and execution of a former Indian naval officer is likely to have jolted India's intelligence agencies.

To stop such a situation from happening again, India could develop its own predictive policing system. India could then deploy this system to identify Indian citizens who may be arrested abroad. India is already developing predictive policing technology. In 2016, the New Delhi police force, in partnership with the Indian Space Research Organization (ISRO), India's equivalent of NASA, developed software called "Crime Mapping, Analytics and Predictive System" (CMAPS). It makes use of satellites to map crime and then decide where to deploy resources to stop future crimes. [145] At the same time, by the end of 2018, every state in India will have access to huge pools of data and analytics that will allow local police forces to not only map crime patterns and deploy resources, but also predict future crimes.[146] States in India are also creating public policy to guide predictive policing deployment. In March 2018, the state of Maharashtra disclosed it was working on a "predictive policing policy".[147]

If India had an advanced predictive policing system in 2016 and preemptively informed the alleged spy that he was going to be targeted in Iran or Pakistan, it may have changed what happened. But India using predictive policing to stop its nationals from being arrested brings its own geopolitical consequences.

If the Pakistani government continuously fails to capture Indian nationals/spies because these people are always "one step ahead", the government will want to know how. Should it find out that India is using predictive policing to keep its nationals out of Pakistan's hands, Pakistan might respond in kind. Pakistan might deploy its own predictive policing system that warns certain Pakistani nationals of arrests in India.

Except, in the case of Pakistan, who will this system be informing?

India has long been the victim of repeated terrorist attacks from militants originating from Pakistan. The worst attack cumulated in 2008, known as 26/11, when ten terrorists took hold of various buildings throughout Mumbai. They killed 164 people. [148] The terrorists originated from Karachi, Pakistan, and they hijacked a boat to enter India.

In the future, when Pakistan has a predictive policing system, it may indirectly support an attack on India by supplying militants with this system. Now militants may be "one step ahead" of the Indian police. This could allow them to evade authorities long enough to carry out an attack.

Will India perceive this as Pakistan explicitly supporting terrorism in India? It is possible that the Pakistani government itself may not be involved at all. It may be militant or terrorist groups based in Pakistan that have purchased a predictive policing system on the black market. These groups may be using the AI to hurt India. The AI would be doing all of the work, from crunching data, identifying risks, and communicating these risks to the militants. Like with North Korea, Pakistan may have purchased its predictive policing system from abroad. Now, the country that sold the AI system to Pakistan may risk becoming involved in the geopolitical spat.

Predictive policing is not just geopolitical for what it can do within borders, but also for what it can do outside borders.

Tracking Crime and Unrest In Another Country

Another way countries might use predictive policing systems is by predicting crime in other countries. Because AI is borderless, it could mean that policing soon becomes borderless. This is similar to the idea of "Predictive Foreign Policy", which was explored in "Next Geopolitics: The Future of World Affairs (Technology) Volume One".

In June 2018, Israel unveiled that it had thwarted 200 attacks through predictive policing. Law enforcement had monitored social media, crunched data, and applied algorithms that identified people who may be planning an attack. Israel then tracked these people to make sure they would not attack the country.[149] In the coming years, Israel may expand its predictive policing to watch for threats in other countries. One of these countries may be Saudi Arabia.

If Israel is alerted by its AI that there is an imminent attack in Saudi Arabia, it will force Tel Aviv to make a decision. Do they share this threat with Riyadh or keep it to themselves?

While Israel and Saudi Arabia are not allies, they have a mutual adversary: Iran. Because of this, they are working together behind the scenes. To take this "secret relationship" to the next level, Israel could share its prediction about crime with Riyadh. By sharing the prediction, Israel may save lives in Saudi Arabia.

But things could also go a different way.

Israel may be preparing for a future where Iran is no longer its main adversary, but Saudi Arabia is. If Israel is working toward this direction, it may choose not to share its prediction with Saudi Arabia. This is a geopolitical risk. If Saudi Arabia finds out that Israel withheld such a prediction, it may view this as a deliberate move by Israel to hurt Saudi Arabia.

Israel though may have bigger plans.

Instead of sharing the prediction with Saudi Arabia, Israel may decide to support those carrying out the crime. Perhaps the crime is large-scale protests against the royal family, which is illegal in Saudi Arabia. [150] Israel may want to remove the ruling family from power and have a new regime take control. Israel could identify the groups carrying out the protests and support them. One way Israel could help them is by launching cyber attacks on Saudi Arabia's military and law enforcement systems as the protests begin, providing "cover" for the protests to spread.

Not only would Saudi Arabia be furious if it found out Israel was supporting the protests, it would also put the Middle East and the US in a tricky position. Two of the most important countries in the region are in direct confrontation with one another because of AI.

Conclusion

Predictive policing could cause policing and geopolitics to converge for the first time.

Whether this means certain people are targeted because of geopolitical tensions or that nations export predictive policing systems to expand their global reach, predictive policing could soon affect relationships between countries.

Predictive policing is not just a risk for governments. It is also a threat for businesses. When AI arrests a business executive over future crimes, businesses will have to think about what to do: do they support the executive and provide legal counsel or do they distance themselves? Do they oppose the government or quietly continue with their operations?

The most dangerous part of predictive policing is the way in which AI decides who is a criminal and who is not.

Could an exchange student who posts radical thoughts about capitalism and the failure of democracy online be arrested for future terrorism? Or could a war veteran, owning several guns and browsing websites having to do with racist and xenophobic content, be arrested for future hate crimes? These possibilities highlight the new kind of society people may have to adjust to.

It is possible that politics in a particular country will force governments to disband and remove predictive policing systems.

And this could mean that in a world governed by AI, those countries without predictive policing could be the safest - both at home and around the world.

Chapter 9
AI Trade

Beijing, China
2036

In 2035, China and the African Union (AU) start negotiations on a new trade deal. If successful, it will connect the world's largest economy (China) with the world's largest trade zone (the AU).

However, the AU is made up of 54 countries, each with a distinct economy. To ensure the trade deal gives China equal access to all of the AU, Beijing appoints AI as its chief trade negotiator.

For China, AI will work out the terms and conditions of the trade deal with the AU.

The world is stunned. Never before has a trade deal been negotiated this way.

As talks begin, China's AI proposes terms and conditions that jolt the AU. This is because, unlike human negotiators, China's AI is predicting events and modeling the trade deal based on these predictions. For example, China's AI predicts that in 2042, demand for SUVs in Gabon will increase by 30%. The AI inputs a condition that in 2042, Gabon buys 60% of its SUVs from Chinese car companies. At the same time, the AI predicts that in 2037, a major drought will hit Lesotho. The AI inputs a condition that in 2037, Lesotho must buy 40% of its fresh water from China and have Chinese firms build at least two desalinization plants in southern Africa.

The AU struggles to negotiate with China's AI. At the same time, other countries like the US, Japan, and India lobby the AU to pull out of trade talks with China. These countries worry that their businesses could be hurt by the conditions China's AI is proposing.

However, the AU continues working on the trade deal. The main reason is because in 2030, the Shanghai Cooperation Organization (SCO), which includes China, Russia, India, Pakistan, Iran and several other countries, created a free trade bloc. By signing with China, the AU also gets access to those markets.

In 2036, China and the AU finalize and implement the trade deal. It is hailed as a great achievement for both sides.

But Beijing shocks the AU when it announces that the same AI which negotiated the trade deal will now manage the trade deal.

The AU is apprehensive.

AI is in charge of its most important trade deal. And there is no telling what it will do.

Introduction

Trade has been the most powerful way for countries to grow their economy and global influence. For example, take China's growing economic power and US-China trade. In 1985, when China was not a leading economy, US-China trade was zero (no deficit). By 2002, as talk of China's economic rise intensified, the US trade deficit with China had reached $100 billion. By 2017, the US trade deficit with China stood at $347 billion.[151]

In other words, as China's economic power grew, its trade relationship with the US (and many other countries) changed. For China, this change was extremely positive. For the US and the rest of the world, it meant that "made in China" goods were entering the market on an unprecedented scale.

What happened between the US and China is an example of what will take place in the future as the global economy changes. At the same time, as new economic powers emerge, the world will experience a major shift in regards to which countries matter.

In 2008, the world's largest economies were (in order): the US, Japan, Germany, China, the United Kingdom, France, Italy, Spain, Canada, and Brazil. The US alone was 26.7% of the global economy.

By 2050, the world's largest economies will be (in order): China, India, the US, Indonesia, Brazil, Russia, Mexico, Japan, Germany, and the United Kingdom. [152] Together, China and India will represent 30.5% of the global economy. [153] Interestingly, in 1820, China and India represented almost 50% of the global economy which may mean that China and India are not emerging powers but they are "re-emerging powers".

As a new world order emerges, the "old and new" will clash. As this happens, trade will be scrutinized more than ever before. Nations will seek to reduce trade deficits, support local firms over foreign firms and ensure their economy can keep up with everyone else.

As nations seek to do these things and more, they might turn to AI. It may be AI that defines how nations trade. And it may even be the trade of AI that defines how countries form new alliances and partnerships.

AI may bring new variables to trade. AI may predict trade events that scare governments. This could anger certain countries while helping others at the same time. As AI manages trade, global power could change in unprecedented ways.

AI To Level The Playing Field Between Mexico And India

Under the traditional model of trade, size mattered more than anything else.

Because of this, smaller economies have started banding together to negotiate trade deals more fairly. In December 2015, the Association of Southeast Asian Nations (ASEAN), a grouping of ten countries in Southeast Asia, such as Vietnam, Indonesia, Thailand and Malaysia, launched the ASEAN Economic Community (AEC). The AEC is an economic union and a single market, much like the European Union (EU). It is made up of more than 600 million people and if calculated as a single economy, would be the seventh largest economy in the world. [154] Alongside giving members better access to each other's markets, the AEC also gives members a stronger foundation to negotiate trade deals. Before the AEC, members negotiated trade deals on their own. Now, through the AEC, member states can negotiate from a united front.

But banding together has its drawbacks.

For one, there might not be AEC-type blocs everywhere. Secondly, countries might not want to have an overarching authority, like ASEAN or the EU, controlling their trade policy. They may want to retain their independence. Third, even if countries are part of AEC-type blocs, they might want a better way to negotiate and manage trade.

Could AI be the answer?

In the future, Mexico and India could move to sign a free trade deal. By 2050, Mexico will be one of the top ten largest economies, with its economy worth $6.863 trillion. India's economy on the other hand will be worth $44.128 trillion. Because of this huge economic gap, under the traditional model of trade, India may have called the shots.

But through AI, Mexico may be able to level the playing field.

What does AI managing trade mean? It could mean that an AI system is in charge of trade. Or it could mean that an AI clone is in charge of trade. In July 2018, a Swiss bank unveiled an AI clone of its chief economist. It has a digital body that mimics the body of the real economist. People can hold conversations with the AI clone. The clone can also give advice.[155]

Similarly, Mexico may decide to create an AI clone of a real trade negotiator or create an AI clone that combines the knowledge of several trade negotiators. Then Mexico could deploy this AI to work on a trade deal with India.

The way AI negotiates trade will be different from people. Mexico's AI might start creating a trade blueprint, not just based on what is happening today, but what it predicts is possible in the coming years.

For example, Mexico's AI might predict that in 2029, climate change could cause widespread drought and famine across parts of India. Between 2029 and 2032, India may be forced to provide basic food rations and supplies to hundreds of millions of people. Mexico may want to be the main supplier of the food and supplies. Therefore, Mexico might include a condition in the trade blueprint that between 2029 and 2032, India must purchase 40% of the food rations and supplies from Mexico and pay a certain price.

Mexico's AI could include more predictions in the trade blueprint.

It might predict that in 2038, the per capita GDP of India's middle class will reach a point where the average family will have more disposable income. Therefore, Mexico's AI might create a condition that in 2038, India increases the imports of dozens of luxury items from Mexico by 200%.

Mexico's AI might even create conditions around the business of AI itself. It could predict that in 2026, 60% of people in India will have AI smartphones. Because of this, India must buy $200 million worth of AI services from Mexican companies.

How would India's government deal with trade being negotiated this way?

India's government will be forced to negotiate a trade deal with AI that makes "wild" predictions about what may or may not happen. Will India agree with the predictions that Mexico's AI is making? Will India produce its own counter-predictions?

India may purposefully not want to discuss the predictions. By not discussing the predictions, India may have more freedom to trade the way it wants.

If India works with Mexico's AI and accepts some of the conditions the AI proposes, it will reflect a new reality. AI would have changed the balance of the Mexico-India relationship. AI would have leveled the playing field for Mexico even though India's economy would be several times larger than Mexico's.

However, negotiating the trade agreement is just one part of the trade deal.

The next part is the actual application of the trade deal.

Mexico, seeing how well its AI negotiated the trade deal, might also direct its AI to manage its trade relationship with India. Now, as trade between Mexico and

India grows, Mexico's AI could start finding problems or taking steps.

Mexico's AI may find problems in the trade deal with India. But Mexico's AI might also find opportunities.

For example, Mexico could feed data on its economy, world events, and financial shifts into its AI. With all this data, Mexico's AI could start taking trade action against India. Textile imports from India might be halted at the border for two weeks because Mexico's AI predicts consumer demand will fall and it does not want excess textile imports in the country. Or, the AI might alert Mexican agriculture companies to export 40% more of a certain vegetable because a weather event in India will create more demand. And Mexico's AI could tell Mexican agriculture companies to lower the price of the vegetable by $0.08 to beat other exporters.

Will India see Mexico's AI as infringing upon the free trade agreement? How will India raise the issue when the "person" India approaches is the AI itself?

AI controlling what comes into the country is already being developed in South Korea. In March 2017, South Korea's customs agency announced that it is building a system that uses AI (along with big data and blockchain) to spot illegal items at the border or in airports.[156] While South Korea is using AI to control imports for public safety, Mexico might do it to support its economy.

India might see what Mexico is doing with AI as "highly effective". New Delhi could introduce its own AI to manage its trade relationship with Mexico.

AI systems working together to manage trade would redefine how nations export and import goods. It could result in a trade boom, because the AI systems find innovative ways to work together. Or it could result in trade breaking down, because the AI systems oppose each other and constantly clash.

The future of trade agreements may not depend on the history of the countries or the difference in economic size. It may depend on how AI interprets the future and how governments react to this interpretation.

When AI Manages Trade Between Several Countries

While AI managing trade between Mexico and India comes with its own challenges, things become even more complicated if a trade bloc or trade group deploys AI to manage trade between members. How will AI make decisions? Will some nations benefit more than others?

One bloc that may turn to AI is the EU.

The EU is the world's most powerful economic union. But in recent years, because of immigration and economic slowdown, the cohesiveness of the EU has been tested. To bring EU members together and make the EU more competitive, the EU has been pursuing leadership in AI. In April 2018, two-dozen members of the EU came together and signed a declaration to develop a "European approach" to AI.[157] Also in April 2018, a group of scientists proposed the creation of AI labs to compete with the US and China. The labs would be called "European Lab for Learning and Intelligent Systems" (Ellis) and would have locations throughout Europe. Ellis is being modeled after CERN, the particle accelerator in Switzerland, which was established after World War II to stop physics experts from leaving Europe.[158]

To become an AI leader, the EU might take a radical approach to AI, such as deploying AI to manage trade between member states and between the EU and the world. The EU may feel that AI can streamline trade and remove barriers, corruption, and bureaucracy.

However, the EU's AI could start creating problems as well.

For example, the AI might spot that Spain, Italy, and France have unequal wine exports. France may have 40% more wine exports than Spain and Italy. The AI could view this as unfair to Spain and Italy.

AI that can spot problems is being developed today.

In May 2018, the EU unveiled a new data protection framework called the "General Data Protection Regulation" (GDPR). The goal of GDPR is to protect the data of people and businesses in the EU. To do this, the GDPR also regulates AI. It has a section which deals with "automated individual decision-making". [159] Essentially, the GDPR wants to ensure that algorithms that make assessments about people do not infringe on people's rights and freedoms.

The GDPR has created a new challenge for companies who deploy algorithms. Ironically, an AI system has been built to help companies. It scans their privacy policies to see whether they comply with the GDPR. [160] In other words, AI is finding issues with what companies are doing.

Similarly, the EU's AI may find problems with what countries are doing - in this case, wine exports from Spain, Italy, and France.

The EU's AI could seek to "equalize" wine exports. The AI, acting with authority from the EU government, could tell the French government to reduce wine exports by 20%. At the same time, the AI could inform the Spanish and Italian governments to increase wine exports by 20%. How would France react to this?

The AI might then move to Germany. It might find that the majority of exports going from Western to Eastern Europe originate from Germany. The AI might see Germany as having a "monopoly" over this trade route. It could then instruct the German government to start creating "trade baskets" that include goods from other Western European members, giving those countries more access to Eastern Europe. How would Germany react to this?

In either case, the EU's AI would be constraining some economies while elevating others. How will the constrained economies feel? Will they see what the AI is doing as illegal? Could France and Germany ignore the AI, in turn ignoring the EU government?

How AI manages trade could cause EU members to diverge. For example, in the case of wine exports from France, Spain and

Italy, France might ignore the AI. In retaliation, the Spanish and Italian governments might begin to limit French wine imports. As AI finds problems, like unequal wine exports, governments will be alerted to problems they did not know existed. As governments take steps to solve these problems, it could create new trade tensions.

Things could get more complicated if AI starts to define trade differently, by including variables that have never been included before.

For example, the movement of people.

The EU's AI might decide to view immigrants as a kind of trade flow.

Currently, the flow of immigration within the EU is largely from Eastern and Central Europe to Western Europe (east to west). The AI may start monitoring this and realize that majority of people from countries like Croatia, Romania, and Bulgaria are resettling in Germany or the Netherlands.

The AI might see this as an unfair economic and social "burden" on Germany and the Netherlands. The AI may try to ensure immigrants resettle equally across the region.

Could the AI start "helping" people from Croatia, Romania, and Bulgaria settle in France, Spain, Italy, and Portugal? The AI might start informing local border security and immigration officers in Germany and the Netherlands to reject people from Croatia, Romania, and Bulgaria once a certain threshold is reached (i.e. 45,000). Or, the AI could start offering "packages", approved by the EU government, to Croatians, Romanians and Bulgarians, like a three-month accommodation, to get them to move to France, Spain, Italy or Portugal.

Germany and the Netherlands may welcome this. But France, Spain, Italy, and Portugal may not want to house these newcomers. In fact, they may have been happy with how things were in the past, when most immigrants settled in Germany and the Netherlands.

Off course, the AI would be challenging EU rules, such as the free movement of people, but considering many EU members are already taking steps to control immigration, the AI may simply be doing what could become the norm in the future.

The AI might even go beyond this. It might start viewing people as a new kind of export.

However, unlike traditional exports, such as cars or wine, the AI might view people as far more valuable and costly. After all, people need housing, jobs, food, and emergency services. If the EU's AI views people as an export, it might introduce new tariffs and taxes.

For example, the AI could create a "human tariff" and apply it to countries that are "exporting" lots of people.

If people are viewed as an export, then trade will be calculated differently. When assessing trade between Germany and Lithuania, the AI might calculate that 40% of Lithuania's exports to Germany are people, not goods.

The AI might see this as a major trade imbalance. More people from Lithuania may be settling in Germany than vice-versa. And Germany may be unable to fully recover the costs of supporting new Lithuanian immigrants.

To balance trade, the AI might set a threshold of how many Lithuanians can move to Germany every year (i.e. 20,000). Once this threshold of 20,000 is reached, the AI could start to penalize the Lithuanian government for every citizen that moves to Germany, such as $10,000 per immigrant after the 20,000 threshold is reached.

In other words, the movement of Lithuanian people, which the AI sees as an export, could result in the Lithuanian government getting fined. How would

Lithuania (or any other country) react to this?

Lithuania might direct its citizens not to move to Germany. But the AI could apply its human tariffs throughout the EU. Germany may not be the only country where people from Lithuania are restricted. The AI may set up different thresholds, such as 20,000 in Germany, 15,000 in France and 7,000 in the Netherlands. As Lithuanian nationals move to these countries and the thresholds are reached, the Lithuanian government could incur huge fines and costs.

Could viewing people as an export force Lithuania to start limiting where its citizens go? Could Lithuania only allow 50,000 people to leave the country every year? This would be a huge shift in the basic freedoms that people have grown to expect.

Alternatively, Lithuania may grow agitated with the EU government and its human tariffs. This could force Lithuania and other affected countries to leave the EU altogether. In other words, as AI views people as a variable of trade, it might lead to the next Brexit.

Separate challenges emerge if AI is managing trade between the EU and another country.

In September 2017, a free trade agreement between Canada and the EU went into effect, called the "Comprehensive Economic and Trade Agreement" (CETA), allowing 98% of Canadian goods to enter the EU without tariffs (only 25% were allowed before CETA). It also allows Canadian firms to put in proposals for EU government work, something that was not possible before.[161] Equally important is that CETA is being viewed as a "blueprint" for future trade deals that Canada could sign with other countries.[162]

Just as the EU may deploy AI to manage trade between EU members, the EU may also deploy AI to manage trade externally. One relationship the AI may manage is between Canada and the EU.

The foundation for this is already being laid down in Singapore.

In May 2018, several organizations in Asia partnered to develop a new AI system that will manage trade at the Port of Singapore, one of the world's busiest ports. The system's main focus is on predicting congestion, accidents, and vessel numbers, to better improve efficiency and safety.[163]

The EU could deploy a similar system in the future to manage European ports.

The AI could work with vessels, both manned and unmanned, to reduce congestion, speed up how ships offload cargo, and reduce accidents. The AI could control unmanned vessels once they enter a certain radius. The AI might also inform vessels about the best time to leave for Europe.

In other words, AI could begin managing Europe's maritime trade.

Many vessels entering European ports may originate from Canada.

But over time, Canada may realize that its vessels are running into "strange" problems. Canadian vessels might repeatedly be told to slow down or back off as vessels from Saudi Arabia, China, and India are given priority. Or Canadian vessels may be told to leave days or weeks later than usual. Canadian vessels might also be told to offload their cargo at ports in less busy parts of Europe. As this happens, Canadian businesses might start reporting that their sales in Europe are dropping.

If such events took place when humans managed trade, Canada would raise it with the EU trade ambassador. But when AI is managing trade, who will Canada raise the issue with, and more importantly, who will Canada blame?

Canada will want to know why the EU's AI system is behaving this way. What if Canada finds out that the EU's AI system is working to give China, India, and Saudi Arabia more priority. Why? Because the EU's AI system may be trying to align the EU with new economic powers. The EU's AI may not value Canadian exports the same way it values exports from China, India, and Saudi Arabia. How would Canada deal with AI thinking and operating this way?

Things get even more confusing and complicated if the EU did not develop the AI system itself. It may have been purchased from another country.

For example, Australia's Department of Defense purchased an AI system from a US technology services company. The system collates data to find patterns and insights.
Instead of creating its own AI, the Australian government decided to purchase AI from the US.[164]

EU officials might have the same attitude and task a company from outside the EU to build the AI trade system. This potentially ropes a third country into a future Canada-EU row.

As AI manages trade, it may redefine what variables are included in trade. At the same time, AI could take steps to help its owner (such as the EU), align with the global economy of tomorrow, angering other nations.

When Nations Trade AI With Each Other

So far, AI trade has revolved around AI managing trade between countries. But AI trade is also about the trade of AI itself and how nations could use the export/import of AI as a tool of geopolitics.

In May 2018, a US technology company unveiled an AI that works as an assistant. It can make phone calls and book appointments, all while talking with real humans and adapting to different conversation styles. The US technology company could use this AI in many different ways, including integrating it into a smartphone operating system and offering it for free to users.

The US firm might also take a different route. It could charge $10 a month for the AI and offer it to the world as a new, AI secretary. This would make the AI service a new AI export from the US.

While the US firm may view its AI as a new business opportunity, the US government might view the AI and other AI services from the US as a new geopolitical opportunity.

The US may decide to create a basket of AI services that the US can offer to select nations around the world. The US may want to use these AI services as a way to bring countries into its sphere of influence.

One of these countries might be India.

For several years, US foreign policy towards India has changed positively. But since 2017, with a new administration in the White House, several major changes have taken place in a short period of time. One of the major changes is the language the US government has used towards Asia. Traditionally, Asia has been referred to as "Asia-Pacific". However, since 2017, the US government has been referring to Asia as the "Indo-Pacific". The reason for this is that "Indo" refers to India. Another change is how the US military is renaming itself to become more "pro-India". In May 2018, the US renamed its pacific command to the "Indo-Pacific Command". According to the US, this was to highlight India's growing role in the region.[165]

As the US looks to take its relationship with India to the next level, could it offer India a basket of AI services?

With AI projected to add more than $15 trillion to the global economy by 2030, India may view the AI basket from the US as new "economic fuel". And if military AI is part of the basket, it could give India a new way to deal with regional threats.

AI from the US then could change the balance of power in South Asia. Yesterday, the balance of power changed because of missile defense systems. Tomorrow, it might change because of AI.

While the US might find favorable footing in India, it could run into problems in other countries, like Malaysia. Like many other countries in Asia, Malaysia is slowly becoming an economic power. Countries looking to grow their hegemony in Asia may compete to bring Malaysia into their corner.

The US might approach Malaysia with a similar deal to that with India. However, while the US may have been the only country offering AI to India, the US may have to compete in Malaysia. Countries like China, Japan, Russia, Israel and perhaps even India, may also be offering Malaysia their AI.

Whose AI will Malaysia choose? Does AI from the US stand a chance?

The US may be late to the game in Malaysia. In January 2018, when Malaysia wanted to turn Kuala Lumpur into a smart city, it bought AI from a Chinese multinational. [166] And in February 2018, when Malaysia wanted to give its police new capabilities, it bought facial recognition technology from a Chinese startup.[167]

If China is the dominant AI power in Malaysia, how can the US succeed?

One way the US can succeed in Malaysia (and other countries) is by redefining how AI is traded. Instead of selling AI as part of a single deal, the US could launch the world's first "AI Free Market" or AIFM. Unlike traditional free markets which revolve around the trade of machinery or agriculture, an AIFM would be a free market that revolves around the trade of AI. Countries that the US invites into its AIFM could share, trade, and sell AI with other members. Perhaps the US would mandate that in certain instances, member states use AI from the US.

The next set of US allies could be those countries that the US invites into its AIFM. And, by mandating the use of its AI in certain instances, the US could ensure that countries remain grounded in US technology.

For a country like Malaysia, being part of the US AIFM could be far more valuable than signing a single agreement with China, Russia, Japan, or India. In fact, Malaysia might be able to get the AI from Japan and India by joining the US AIFM (Japan and India may be members).

Could a US AIFM be the next iteration of the International Monetary Fund (IMF) or

World Bank, both of which were started by the US after World War II? Will the US allow its adversaries, like China or Russia, into its AIFM, the same way it allowed China and Russia into the IMF and World Bank?

The next important meeting of heads of state might not be when the G20 or BRICS meet, but when AIFM members meet to discuss the future.

A separate set of challenges emerges if countries face obstacles in exporting their AI.

For example, in the case of the US and India, New Delhi might accept the US basket of AI innovations or join the US AIFM. But after a few years, India might approach the US with its own AI. India might want to sell its AI to US firms. But the US might view India's AI as a threat to its own AI companies.

The next trade tensions between the US and India then might not be over tariffs on Harley Davison motorcycles[168] but over India trying to export AI to the US. If India cannot get its AI into the US, it may start to view its relationship with the US as one-sided.

Perhaps another country might view this as a geopolitical opportunity. Russia might approach India and offer Indian AI firms unrestricted access to the Russian market as a way to win support from New Delhi. Will India accept such an offer? Will the US rethink its decision if Russia makes such an offer? Could Russia launch its own AIFM?

In the future, who governments purchase AI from or sell AI to could be a new indicator of geopolitical alignment and support.

Conclusion

Trade and economic power has always been interlinked. The more economic power a country has, the more they could bend trade to their will. The more a country could bend trade to their will, the more economic power a country has.

But since the end of World War II, trade and economic power has remained concentrated in a handful of countries. These countries have set the agenda for the global economy. Slowly, a new world order is emerging and trade and economic power might begin to move in a different direction.

As nations seek to forge new trade agreements, they might look toward AI to help (along with blockchain). In the future, AI could be more advanced than people in many aspects, making AI a powerful and effective manager of trade.

Challenges will of course emerge. How much responsibility will countries give to AI? Will AI make decisions around trade that fractures relations? How will AI work with other AIs to manage a trade relationship?

And of course, there will be some countries that continue to use people for trade. Perhaps they prefer doing so or perhaps they are forced to use people because they do not have AI.

These differences, while important, take attention away from the bigger picture.

The future global economy may not depend on currency or gold. The future global economy might not depend on how businesses operate, how banks invest money or how governments create policy.

The future of the global economy and trade could depend on how AI interprets and adapts to what it believes is on the horizon.

Chapter 10
AI Education

Moscow, Russia
2038

In 2030, a new era of education begins.

The US develops the world's first downloadable skills technology. Instead of learning skills over months or years, people can download subjects in seconds. Everything from how to fly a plane to advanced chemistry can be downloaded in an instant and learned. Underlying this technology is AI. It advises people about what to learn and in some cases creates brand new skills and subjects for people to download.

In 2032, Russia develops the same technology. Russia subsidizes it and offers it to its population for a small fee. At the beginning, most "early adopters" in Russia are the youth. Because Russia developed the technology after the US, most of the downloadable skills originate from the US.

The early adopters in Russia, measuring in the tens of thousands, download everything they can. And, by 2034, Russia's economy is booming. Downloadable skills have given birth to highly disruptive startups and huge scientific breakthroughs.

However, at the same time, protests are growing in Russia.

By 2038, the protests become violent. More than 30,000 people begin protesting in Moscow and St. Petersburg, demanding an end to the Russian government and the political system.

The Russian government, worried about what is taking place, starts analyzing what caused these protests to begin. Russia realizes that many of protestors are the "early adopters". Russia then analyzes the skills these people downloaded. Russia discovers that deep within the code are hidden layers. These layers are filled with Western ideologies and beliefs.

In other words, as people in Russia downloaded skills from the US, they were not just getting skills in the package. They were also downloading political beliefs and ideologies that influenced their opinions about Russia.

Russia and much of the world is shocked at this level of US intrusion.

Russia forces its early adopters to download new skills. These new skills are explicitly pro-Russian. The US plan for Russia has failed.

Because of downloadable skills and AI, people in Russia have become more opposed to the US than ever before.

Introduction

How would societies and economies look if people could download skills in a matter of seconds or minutes?

While the idea of downloading skills may seem "out there", the reality is that several organizations are already working on this technology.

In March 2016, the US Pentagon's Defense Advanced Research Projects Agency (DARPA) unveiled a project called "Targeted Neuroplasticity Training" (TNT). The goal of TNT is to make the brain learn faster through "downloadable learning" - rapidly downloading skills, like a language, by putting the brain in the right state. [169] In February 2016, a research firm in California announced that they had developed a way to "upload skills" to the brain. Their technology takes the electrical signals of a person's brain and then feeds those signals to someone else. This is known as "Transcranial Direct Current Stimulation" (TDCS). In one test, the electrical signals of six pilots were sent to a group of people with no flying experience. When the group that received the pilot's signals completed a flight simulation, it performed 33% better than the group that received no signals. [170] In December 2011, researchers from the US and Japan showed that they could activate certain parts of the brain in a pre-recorded way. The lead researcher said that such breakthroughs could allow people to learn skills, like playing the piano, with "little to no conscious effort".[171]

These advances represent the biggest transformation in the way people learn. No longer will people have to go through years of schooling or training to learn a specific skill or set of skills. Instead, they may be able to download what they need, when they need it. As downloadable skills become a reality, the backbone of this technology could be AI. It could be AI that acts as the operating system (OS) and even designs and develops brand new skills for people to learn.

As downloadable skills technology emerges, it could divide the world in a new way. Certain countries might have this technology and refuse to share it with the rest of the world. Or those with malicious intent could force people to download skills, brainwashing them. How people learn in the future could soon become geopolitical.

AI-Based Education: The Next Developmental Divide

By 2030, the biggest company on the Internet could be an education platform, using "robot teachers".[172] In the age of social media, the possibility that a digital school could become the dominant force on the Internet seems unthinkable. But with the ability to download skills on the horizon, it may be possible.

When it comes to AI's role in downloading skills, the main use of AI could be to act as the new counselor. AI could tell someone what skills they should download based on what a person wants.

AI might show a 34-year-old single mother how to manage an AI fund in Cambodia if she wants to be successful in Southeast Asia. Or AI could teach a 24-year-old carpenter how to develop and program physical robots if he wants to make more than $100,000 in the next 12 months. Or AI could demonstrate to a newly-wed couple how to use CRISPR for agriculture if they want to do charity in Ethiopia.

AI might also go beyond telling people what to learn and could start to create entirely new skills. For example, AI could create a skill for becoming a strategist for financial systems in VR-worlds. Or AI could create a skill for becoming a botanist for the moons of Jupiter.

As downloadable skills technology emerges, it could divide the world in a new way.

Certain countries might have this technology. Others might not. Having downloadable skills technology may be as important for countries as having Internet and electricity access.

Because several organizations in the US are working on downloadable skills, the US may become the first country in the world to have this technology. This means the US could soon be in control of a technology the whole world wants.

Could the US use downloadable skills technology to expand its geopolitical power?

Initially, the US might approach downloadable skills technology from a business point of view. US firms may offer downloadable skills to the highest bidder - the 1% of US society. This would exacerbate a separate kind of divide: the one between the rich and poor. But there is another possibility. The US government may see a huge potential in downloadable skills technology to transform US society and give the US a competitive edge over the rest of the world. The more "enlightened" the US population becomes, the more they may contribute to the economy. The US government could begin subsidizing this technology and offer it exclusively to its people.

As people in the US download skills, they might take their new knowledge abroad.

For example, after downloading advanced skills, dozens of US entrepreneurs might start businesses in India. By 2050, India will be the second largest economy in the world and the US entrepreneurs may want to capitalize on this. [173] Thanks to downloadable skills, not only could the US entrepreneurs have a deep understanding of India's business landscape but they may also speak local dialects, know the legal system and intellectual property law, and understand the local customs and norms. The US entrepreneurs may have more awareness, knowledge and understanding of India than any other foreigners and many locals in India.

At the same time, the US entrepreneurs may have skills that nobody else in the world has, including people in India. For example, thanks to downloadable skills technology, the US entrepreneurs may understand how to create digital currencies that have AI embedded in them, allowing currencies to "think" on their own, including converting themselves or changing where they are invested. In other words, currencies themselves could be the new investment bankers. In the future, such an industry could be incredibly lucrative in India. But because nobody else has the skills, US entrepreneurs would be able to dominate this industry. US entrepreneurs would be profiting and dominating an industry in a way no local Indian can. How would the Indian government feel about this? Perhaps India will see this as a new wave of colonization as US entrepreneurs "take over" India's economy.

As people from the US succeed in India and other parts of the world thanks to downloadable skills, governments may begin to call on the US to share/sell this technology. Will the US comply? Why should they?

The US has a similar leadership with AI-chips. Today, US technology firms develop the most advanced AI-chips in the world.[174] The rest of the world depends on US AI-chips. The US does not share its patent or designs for AI-chips with anyone and this gives the US a huge advantage in the ongoing AI race.

Why wouldn't the US apply the same logic to downloadable skills technology?

While the US may want to keep its edge with downloadable skills technology, it may be inclined to share the technology if the "right" offer is made.

For example, countries in Africa, like Nigeria, South Africa and Ethiopia, may want downloadable skills technology for their people. Governments in these countries may see this technology as key to educating their populations and transforming their countries. But instead of demanding the US share or sell the technology, these countries may offer the US access to their respective markets in exchange for the technology.

US mining companies may be given exclusive access to rare resources and minerals. US technology firms may be given a monopoly to sell smartphones, self-driving cars, and networking solutions. US financial firms may gain access to sell banking and investment services. All of this would be offered in exchange for downloadable skills technology. Any non-US firm would lose out. Would the US turn down such an offer? By gaining exclusive access to Africa's leading economies, the US could grow its influence on the fastest growing continent in the world.

At the same time, the US may choose to purposefully offer downloadable skills technology to "reorient countries" away from US adversaries.

China is currently driving a multi-trillion dollar initiative called "One Belt, One Road" (OBOR). It seeks to connect countries throughout Asia, Africa, the Middle East and Europe through Chinese infrastructure and technology. Countries in Central Asia are core to OBOR.

In the coming years, China may offer Central Asian nations a combination of electrical grids, fresh water plants, self-driving cars, and AI services. The US may step in and alongside matching what China is offering, the US could offer downloadable skills technology as well. Central Asia may jump at such an opportunity. Countries in Central Asia may view downloadable skills as key to taking their nation into the future. In exchange for downloadable skills technology, the US may demand that Central Asian nations do not partake in OBOR.

If Central Asian nations agree, an entire region of the world could be reoriented away from China and pulled toward the US. How will China deal with its most expensive and grand geopolitical strategy falling apart because of downloadable skills technology?

Rejecting Foreigners To Protect Geopolitical Edge

If the US decides to ban the export of downloadable skills technology (the same way the US has limited the export of military drones in the past), it could fuel something else: downloadable skills tourism.

People from around the world could visit the US to download skills. But this puts the US in a predicament: will the US only allow US citizens to access downloadable skills or will the US allow anyone from anywhere?

The US may decide to allow anyone to take advantage of the technology. Potentially tens of millions of people could come to the US, growing the economy in a new way. But on purpose, the US might restrict certain groups of people from accessing all downloadable skills.

The US may identify a small group of nations that the US considers its biggest geopolitical and economic adversaries. For example: China, Russia, Iran and India. The US may only allow people from these countries access to 10% or 12% of the full downloadable skills catalogue. While people from France, Brazil, Japan, South Korea, and Saudi Arabia may be able to download whatever they want, people from China, Russia, Iran, and India would be significantly restricted in what they can download.

This would be a calculated move by the US to stop people from downloading skills and taking these skills back to their home countries. The US would be trying to protect its competitive edge. This would also be a new kind of US censorship.

Today, China censors the Internet and media to protect its political system. Tomorrow, the US may censor downloadable skills technology to protect its economy.

If select groups of people are being restricted, on purpose, from accessing downloadable skills technology, it could cause alarm bells to ring. The countries where these people come from may see this as a deliberate strategy by the US to disadvantage their people. This could push countries, like China, Russia, Iran, and India to band together and strike back at the US. One way they could do this is by restricting people with downloadable skills from starting businesses, investing in the country or even entering the country. Considering China and India will be the largest economies in the future, losing access to these markets may make people think twice about downloading skills from the US. Of course, there are grey areas here. For one, how will China or India know who has downloaded skills and who has not?

Equally important is the decisions companies will make in the age of downloadable skills. Companies are always looking to acquire the best talent and people with downloadable skills may be the best talent in the future. But if people originating from China, Russia, Iran, and India cannot access all downloadable skills, companies may not hire from these markets. Again, this could rile governments. The Russian government, for example, may ban companies who refuse to hire Russians because they do not possess downloaded skills. This will create a new set of problems between Russia and other countries.

The ability to download skills could push countries to take extreme measures, both to procure the technology and protect their societies from it.

Forget Converting Terrorists, Focus On Downloading Terrorists

Downloadable skills technology will not just give countries a competitive edge.

It will also give certain organizations an edge. This may include terrorist groups.

In January 2016, Europol, the law enforcement agency of the European Union (EU), warned that the Islamic State (IS) was creating "secret training camps" throughout

Europe. According to Europol, these camps were training fighters to conduct "special forces style" assaults. The agency also warned that IS could look to rope in new refugees in these camps.[175]

In the age of downloadable skills, the next terrorist training camps could be entirely different places. Instead of converting people, terrorists could start having people download "terrorist skills". Terrorists could task AI with creating brand new terrorist ideologies, more dangerous and radical than anything that exists today. If people can download skills like how to play a piano or build a rocket, why not skills like "How to Build an EMP Bomb" or an ideology like "Jihad Against the West"? Terrorists downloading skills changes the entire playbook of who is a terrorist or who is at risk of being radicalized. In fact, forceful conversion could take a new form. Terrorists may start forcefully downloading skills into people they have kidnapped. These could be young children, women, or even the elderly. They could have all kinds of propaganda and ideologies forcefully downloaded into them. Once they "awaken", these people may be radicalized terrorists, slaves, or commanders, with only a sliver of who they were before. Then these people could execute terrorist attacks like suicide bombings or mall shootings.

How will governments deal with terrorism spreading this way? To stop downloadable skills from getting into the hands of terrorists, governments could go after the source - the group or country that is creating terrorist skills. If hundreds of people in the United Kingdom are downloading terrorist skills, the United Kingdom will want to know where these "skills" are coming from. Is someone deliberately creating these skills to destabilize British society? Should the United Kingdom find out that it is a country in the Middle East or North Africa, it will place a new challenge in front of London. Not only is British society at risk from terrorists downloading skills but a foreign government is indirectly supporting these terrorists by creating terrorist skills in the first place.

If the situation is grave enough, will the United Kingdom or other countries try to overthrow the foreign government behind the terrorist skills? Will this have any impact in the age of downloadable skills?

At the same time, because downloadable skills are a technology, the group creating terrorist skills might not be in the Middle East or North Africa. They could be in the West. This only complicates how countries deal with future terrorist challenges.

Perhaps the United Kingdom will turn to predictive policing.

It could task AI with identifying people who are at risk of becoming terrorists because of downloadable skills. At the same time, on a global level, the United Kingdom may see a foreign government supporting terrorism through downloadable skills as an "act of war". Could organizations like the North Atlantic Treaty Organization (NATO) get involved? Will Article 5 (if one member state goes to war, all member states go to war) be updated for downloadable skills terrorism? If the situation is severe enough, it might. In May 2017, NATO warned that it could invoke Article 5 if one of its member states was hit by a severe enough cyber attack.[176]

Governments funding terrorism is not new. Except, funding has always revolved around money and arms. If tomorrow, governments fund terrorism through technology, like downloadable skills, it will reconfigure how nations deal with terrorism and where terrorism itself comes from.

Creating Downloadable Skills Courses With Political Undertones

Another geopolitical risk that comes with downloadable skills technology is the way in which governments could seek to undermine other countries.

In 2011, Estonia introduced a law that forced people to speak Estonian or lose their jobs. The law was intended to take Estonia further away from its Soviet past and stop people from speaking Russian.[177]

In the age of downloadable skills, countries may take a different approach to make their population think a certain way. In the future, Estonia may force its people to download certain ideologies and courses if they wish to get a job or if immigrants want to attain citizenship. And these ideologies and courses could be political, such as, "How Russia Destroyed Estonia" or "Why Estonia Needs The West". Estonia could forcefully condition its population to become anti-Russian in a bid to achieve a social and political objective.

Here, Estonia would be using downloadable skills technology to change the way its population thinks. But what if a foreign government wanted to influence the way a foreign population thinks?

If downloadable skills technology is democratized (shared or developed around the world), potentially tens of millions of people around the world could be downloading skills. A portion of these people, such as 100,000 or 200,000 people may be from Russia. But initially, Russian institutions may not be supplying downloadable skills. It may be US institutions. Even though the Russian government may be wary of allowing the US to supply downloadable skills to its people, Moscow may allow it to ensure its people can download skills and stay competitive.

As hundreds of thousands of Russians begin downloading skills designed in the US, they might not just be learning the skills themselves. The skills might be deliberately created to influence other aspects of the person downloading them. US skills, for example, might have "programming" that bolsters capitalism and democracy and plays down communism and Marxism. In other words, the US could deliberately create courses that promote Western ideologies.

The US may call this as an "injection plan". Inject 100,000 or 200,000 people in a country with Western ideologies and these people will naturally spread these ideologies throughout a particular society.

In Russia, tens of thousands of Russians may begin protesting certain laws or violently revolting against Russian politicians and government figures. They may not even fully understand why they are behaving in this way. Consider that unlike traditional learning, which can take months or years to learn, downloadable skills might take just seconds or minutes. People will not necessarily be able to process or understand everything they have downloaded into their mind. They may start to behave or think differently and may not understand why.

If major protests and violent revolts start to shake Russian society, the Russian government may begin to investigate what is happening. It might notice that pushback against the Russian government is growing as more and more Russians download skills from the US. How might Russia react if it finds out that the US has been purposefully manipulating downloadable skills to change how Russians think? This would be foreign interference on a scale Russia and the world has never witnessed.

Russia could view this as brainwashing and as a deliberate attack on Russia. However, before Russia can even respond to the US, it will have to figure out a way to "reverse" what its citizens have learned. Could Russia direct its AI to create courses that not only reverse what Russian citizens have learned, but also make the US appear as an enemy and a bad country?

The next instance of foreign interference might not be over election meddling but over manipulating downloadable skills.

Conclusion

As technology advances, future generations will be downloading skills in ways previous generations only dreamed of.

Certain countries will have newfound power. Certain populations will be enlightened. Less fortunate countries will struggle. Less fortunate populations will have to learn in a classroom.

Again, AI will be the driving force behind all of this. AI will be the OS. AI will be telling people what to download. AI will be creating new skills and subjects. AI may even be working directly with governments to train people in a way that guarantees economic growth.

All of this means that downloadable skills technology may fuel the next renaissance.

The last renaissance took place in cafes and restaurants. It took place as people exchanged ideas and had stimulating conversations. It affected a small percentage of the world's population.

Now, the next renaissance is being developed in boardrooms and labs. It is being developed by engineers, programmers, policy makers and futurists. And it will affect everyone, everywhere.

The big question then is if this new renaissance will spawn the next economic designs, political ideologies, and social constructs - the same way the previous renaissance did. If the next renaissance leads to these changes, it means downloadable skills are far more impactful than anyone realizes.

Downloadable skills are about changing the way people think. And when people think differently, geopolitics, economics, and every other system that governs this world will change in ways nobody can imagine.

Chapter 11
AI Warfare

New Delhi, India
2030

In 2029, amidst rising tensions with Pakistan, India introduces a new military doctrine.

The old doctrine of "no first strike", which guided India since independence, is thrown out. In its place is a new doctrine that gives India the "first strike" option. But only if India's government or AI believes national security to be at risk.

It is the first military doctrine in the world to include AI.

Shortly after this, India deploys more than 5,000 autonomous drones to its border with Pakistan. These drones act as a swarm. They can break into small swarms or can act as a single massive swarm. And they can identify and engage targets without any human input.

It is the third deployment of so called "killer robots", after Israel in 2023 (Gaza Strip) and China in 2026 (South China Sea).

The world holds its breath. If India's AI drones attack Pakistan, it risks a nuclear war.

A year after India's drones are deployed, they attack for the first time.

Analyzing Pakistan's military, India's drones predict that there is an 80% chance that Pakistani insurgents will enter India and conduct terrorist attacks. According to the drones, the insurgents will do this under the cover of fire from Pakistan's military stationed along the Line of Control (LoC). The Indian government gives the drones the green light to protect India. It is left to the drones to decide how to do this.

Immediately, 2,000 drones attack Pakistani military outposts along the LoC, collectively as a swarm. The remaining 3,000 drones spread themselves along the LoC and watch for insurgents. Within 12 minutes, dozens of Pakistan's military outposts are destroyed. And close to 30 insurgents are killed.

The drones communicate with senior military commanders in New Delhi. The drones are told to "put more pressure" on Pakistan. It is left to the drones to decide how to do this as well.

From the LoC, India's drones start to move inland, toward Lahore. The drones believe this is where the insurgents originated from. As the drones move toward Lahore, they encounter Pakistani fighter jets, air defense systems and anti-drone lasers. The drones, acting as dozens of smaller swarms, maneuver themselves, sacrificing some drones and reforming.

By the time India's drones reach Lahore, only 500 are left.

In Lahore, the 500 drones fire all their ammunition and then engage in kamikaze (suicide) attacks.

After a few hours, more than 8,000 people in Pakistan have lost their lives. Many of them are civilians and innocent bystanders.

Pakistan, wounded and furious, declares war on India. In response, India declares war on Pakistan. Hundreds of thousands of soldiers and thousands of fighter jets and tanks are mobilized on either side of the border.

From Asia to Europe to North America, leaders of nations are alerted.

Two nuclear armed states are going to war. And it is all because of AI.

Introduction

The single most discussed and debated area of AI has to do with its weaponization. Will governments allow AI to make military decisions? Will AI be allowed to fire and shoot at targets? Will AI start the next war?

At the beginning of the 21st century, the idea that AI could start wars was truly science fiction. There wasn't enough happening. AI wasn't advanced enough. More than a decade later and AI is slowly reaching a point where it could start the next war around the world.

In May 2018, in the US, the Pentagon's Defense Advanced Research Projects Agency (DARPA) announced a project called "Urban Reconnaissance through Supervised Autonomy" (URSA). The goal of URSA is to allow drones and sensors to autonomously scan a city and decide who is friendly and who is hostile. In other words, AI will tell soldiers who to kill.[178] In March 2018, in China, the People's Liberation Army Ground Forces (PLAGF) tested old Type 59 tanks that were converted into remotely controlled drones. At the time, the PLAGF wanted to integrate AI into the tanks to make them act autonomously.[179] In July 2017, in Russia, an arms maker announced that it was building AI drones that would use AI to identify targets and make decisions.[180]

These advancements in weaponized AI point to a fundamental shift in warfare. In the future, AI may form the next soldiers and commanders. For the first time in history, AI may be partly in control of a military.

This has huge ramifications for geopolitics, peace and security around the world. In the age of AI warfare, no government will know when the next conflict can break out. This makes the future of geopolitics more unpredictable than ever before.

When AI Controls Physical Hardware

In June 2017, a Chinese billionaire warned that AI could start the next world war.

His belief was that every industrial revolution caused a world war. And because the world was in the middle of a new industrial revolution, another world war was on the horizon. The billionaire did stress that if the next world war was started by technology, humans would "ultimately" win.[181]

When someone says AI could start a war, what do they mean?

In science fiction, AI starting a war has to do with AI controlling nuclear weapons and launching them. But that is science fiction. In the real world, instead of nukes, AI may control other weapons and systems. This does not reduce the risks that AI warfare brings. It just changes the way these risks emerge.

One way countries are weaponizing AI is by giving AI control of physical hardware.

In 2008, Israel revealed it was working on a missile defense system that worked through AI. At the time, Israel was preparing for a war with Iran where huge amounts of projectiles would be launched from Iran, and Iranian proxy states, into Israel. In such a situation, Israel wanted a missile defense system that could act autonomously instead of waiting for human commands. [182] A few years later, Israel introduced the famous "Iron Dome" missile system, which has semi-autonomous capabilities. But even the Iron Dome is limited in what it can do. For example, the Iron Dome takes between two to three minutes for a command to be executed.[183] If rockets and shells are being launched into Israel, 'two or three minutes' is a long time for a system to snap into action.

In coming years, to improve its air defenses, Israel may introduce the next version of the Iron Dome. This new version may be fully autonomous and have offensive capabilities, meaning it could defend against incoming threats (like incoming rockets) and launch missiles at targets (like attacking an enemy convoy in another country). Israel may deploy the new Iron Dome system on the ground and at sea (in November 2017, Israel unveiled an operational Iron Dome system for navy ships).[184]

The moment Israel deploys the new Iron Dome system, it will send shockwaves throughout the Middle East and the world.

What kind of decisions will this system make? Governments and businesses in the Middle East would be operating in a permanent state of unpredictability because of AI, not people.

A short time after deploying the new Iron Dome, it might make an offensive decision.

In February 2018, an Iranian drone crossed over into Israel. This was seen as a huge breach of Israeli national security and a shift in the ongoing conflict between Israel and Iran. According to Israel, the drone, which was shot down by an Israeli helicopter, was weaponized (it had explosives).[185]

In 2020 or 2021, a similar event may take place.

Only this time, Israel may have the new version of its Iron Dome system active. How would the AI in this system react to an armed Iranian drone trying to enter Israel? What if the next attack involves a swarm of Iranian drones?

Upon identifying the Iranian drone (or drones), Israel's AI may instantly launch missiles to intercept and destroy them. In fact, Israel's AI may have predicted the drones would try to enter Israel based on various data.

But Israel's AI may go beyond just shooting down the drones.

Israel may have given the AI a "response window". A response window would be a period of time in which the AI can make decisions on its own without asking for approval. Why is there a need for a response window? Because threats are emerging rapidly. Governments may want to give AI the ability to move quickly in high risk situations.

Perhaps Israel gives its AI a response window of five minutes. If a major threat to Israel is expected to take place in under five minutes, the AI can take any action to protect Israel. It does not have to ask the government for permission.

In the situation above involving Iranian drones, Israel's AI may believe that the Iranian drones are just the "first wave". It may believe that within the next four minutes, another attack will take place, this time through shells and rockets being launched from Iranian proxy states. Because the AI is acting within the response window, it will be acting without any human input or control.

Israel's new Iron Dome system may then become offensive and launch missiles at locations throughout Lebanon, Syria, and the Gaza Strip. Dozens of buildings and factories may be hit and destroyed. At the same time, the Iron Dome System may communicate with autonomous unmanned ground vehicles (UGVs) that may be patrolling Israel's ground borders.

The AI may instruct the UGVs to shoot anyone that tries to cross the border in the next hour. The AI may believe that insurgents could try to cross over into Israel as Lebanon, Syria, and the Gaza Strip are attacked.

Israel already has UGVs patrolling its borders. Since February 2016, the Israeli Defense Forces (IDF) has been patrolling the border with Gaza with remotely-controlled trucks. In 2017, they planned to make these trucks completely autonomous [186]. In an interview with a Japanese media outlet, the IDF said that they want to install weapons on these vehicles. According to the Japanese media outlet that conducted the interview, the technology already exists to make the weapons fully autonomous.[187]

Once sites in Lebanon, Syria, and the Gaza Strip are attacked, Israel's AI may reduce the threat level to normal. The UGVs patrolling Israel's borders may revert back to the original behavior. But as the smoke rises, a new reality will be settling in for the Middle East, and the world: AI has just led its first war.

There are multiple layers to this.

First, AI has just rewritten Israeli foreign policy. Before AI, Israel may have never done what it did in Lebanon, Syria, or the Gaza Strip. After AI, Israel's position is completely different. Even if the Israeli government had been quietly working with political parties in Lebanon, Syria, or the Palestinian Territories for peace, it wouldn't matter anymore. The actions of AI would have created a new foreign policy for Israel.

Second, the world will have to decide whether it aligns with Israel's AI or not. This is a brand new decision governments will have to make. In the past, governments have had to side with people; in the future, they may have to side with AI. If certain governments do not side with Israel's AI, such as the Iranian, Iraqi, or Saudi governments, it could lead to a wider conflict in the Middle East.

Thirdly, Israel's AI might have attacked hundreds or thousands of innocent people and bystanders. This creates a major humanitarian component. It is important to note here that AI might "desensitize" warfare. Because AI is in charge, not humans, governments may launch more aggressive military campaigns. If a military campaign fails or results in huge fallout, AI can be blamed.

Equally important is how Israel will justify the actions of its AI.

This question ties all the three layers - foreign policy, alignment and humanitarian - together. Israel will have to justify the actions its AI has made but how will it do this?

Institutions like the United Nations (UN) may demand that Israel justify why its AI believed another attack was going to take place after the Iranian drone was shot down.

Israel may share the data and intelligence that its AI used to make its prediction. But what if a third party, like Norway, runs the same data and intelligence through its own AI and Norway's AI does not predict that another attack will take place? It could mean that Israel's AI is flawed. Or that it has been programmed to be biased and more aggressive towards Iran, Syria, Lebanon, and Palestine.

When discussing AI controlling physical hardware, like a missile defense system, there is a huge grey area over just how governments will "calculate control". In the example above, Israel's new Iron Dome system may be 100% autonomous. But what if Israel made its new system only 25% autonomous?

Questions will emerge as to what this 25% control translates into. Does it mean that 25% of the time, the AI system is in control? If so, nations will want to know at what time is the AI in control. Is it 25% of a standard, 24-hour day or is it 25% of a 12-hour day?

Control may have nothing to do with time and instead means that AI is only in control of 25% of the missile-defense systems capabilities. Different questions will then emerge. What capabilities does the AI control? Does it control a part of the targeting system, the launch system or is it 25% of the entire system?

These questions may seem irrelevant but the degree to which AI controls weapons will ultimately decide what these weapons can do without humans.

AI Cyber Warfare Could Start New Conflicts

When it comes to AI warfare, AI controlling physical hardware is one part of the picture. The other part is the role AI could play in cyber warfare.

AI in the cyber world is just as dangerous as AI in the real world. In fact, AI in the cyber world could be more dangerous because of the amount of people it could affect. If AI launches a cyber attack on the electrical grid of a nation or manipulates the stock market, it could affect tens of millions of people for an indefinite amount of time.

In the cyber world, AI will play a dual role: it will be the defender and the attacker.

In August 2016, DARPA held a "Grand Cyber Challenge". The goal of the challenge was to have different AI systems compete to identify vulnerabilities in a network. [188] Once the vulnerabilities were detected, the AI had to patch them in real time. The groups partaking in the challenge all developed AI systems that could patch networks on their own. But their model could be inverted: instead of patching networks, the AI systems could exploit them.

In other words, AI could be responsible for the next cyber attacks.

In fact, AI cyber attacks may already be taking place.

In November 2017, a US cyber security company reported an attack they had never seen before. One of their clients in India was attacked by a system that used AI. The AI monitored the network of the client and "learned" how real users on the network were behaving. Then it mimicked the behavior of real users. This kind of "machine intelligence" made it harder for the cyber security company to spot the cyber attack.[189]

As AI enters the picture, the kind of cyber attacks that take place could also change. In the past, cyber attacks stole data or crashed systems. In the future, cyber attacks may permanently destroy whatever they target.

The beginning of this was the Stuxnet virus, a first of its kind, uncovered in 2010. Stuxnet was allegedly developed by the US and Israel to counter Iran's nuclear enrichment program. When Stuxnet gained access to Iran's nuclear enrichment facilities, it caused centrifuges to spin out of control. The centrifuges then overheated and destroyed themselves. Within months of Stuxnet, Iran's main nuclear enrichment facility saw the number of active centrifuges drop from 7,052 to 4,592 to 3,936.[190]

Could AI cyber attacks mimic Stuxnet?

There are two levels to this.

The first level is the country-level.

During the historic summit between the US president and North Korean leader on June 12, 2018 in Singapore, cyber attacks on Singapore surged. Between June 11 and June 12, almost 40,000 cyber attacks hit

Singapore, of which 92% were looking for vulnerable devices. The number of cyber attacks on Singapore was 4.5X more than the cyber attacks on the US and Canada during the same days.[191]

While Singapore did not have AI protecting it during the summit, if it did it may have led Singapore into dangerous territory.

That is because, according to cyber security firms, 88% of the cyber attacks on Singapore originated from Russia. Whether or not Russian hackers were responsible or if hackers simply used a proxy in Russia to launch the attacks, if Singapore had an AI system up and running, the AI may have believed Russia was responsible.

Depending on the ethics and programming, Singapore's AI may have retaliated against Russia for the cyber attack. But what will Singapore's AI attack? Singapore's AI may target vulnerable systems in cities like Moscow and St. Petersburg. Singapore's AI may launch sophisticated cyber attacks at these systems that destroy them.

But what will Singapore's AI be destroying? In 2014, the German Federal Office for Information Security (BSI) reported that a major cyber attack targeted a German steel mill. The cyber attack was so powerful that the factory workers were unable to shut down one of the blast furnaces. This caused extensive damage to the steel mill.[192]

If Singapore's AI launches cyber attacks that results in factories in Russia catching fire and people being injured (or even dying), it would put Singapore on a collision course with Russia.

How would Russia respond to Singapore's AI launching cyber attacks like this? Will Singapore stand behind the decisions of its AI? What happens if Russia has its own AI protecting the country from cyber attacks?

Countries thinking about putting AI in charge of cyber security must be ready to accept the decisions the AI makes.

The second level is the regional-level.

AI cyber security could be the new way for nations to partner.

In May 2018, fourteen countries in the Pacific Ocean, including New Zealand, Australia, Fiji, Samoa, Kiribati, and the Marshall Islands, created a new group to improve cyber security. The members of the group will share data and collaborate around cyber security readiness.[193] This is one of the first regional initiatives centered entirely around cyber security.

As this new cyber security group thinks about new ways to develop, could it look toward AI? For example, could the group introduce an AI shield?

This would be a regional cyber security shield that protects members of the group. And it would connect members through AI. The shield would watch for cyber attacks and retaliate against aggressors.

If the cyber security group employs this, it could lead the group into unchartered territory.

In December 2017, New Zealand's Government Communications Security Bureau (GCSB), which is in charge of intelligence collection and analysis in New Zealand, warned that one-third of all cyber attacks on New Zealand may be state-backed. In other words, the GCSB believes that foreign governments are behind a large percentage of cyber attacks on New Zealand.[194]

In 2020 or 2021, New Zealand's cyber security may be managed by the cyber security group's AI shield.

The next time a cyber attack hits New Zealand, it may be deflected by the AI shield. At the same time, the AI may retaliate.

The group members might sign a charter around how the AI should behave if a member state is threatened. If the AI shield retaliates against the cyber attacks on New Zealand, who will it attack?

A large number of cyber attacks on New Zealand may originate from Laos. The AI shield may launch cyber attacks at targets across Laos, from electrical grids to water plants to transportation networks. And the cyber attacks may be intended to permanently destroy systems and infrastructure.

The AI shield will be representing a regional group. When it does something, it will be involving all members. If the AI shield attacks Laos, in retaliation for a cyber attack on New Zealand, it will not just be a fight between New Zealand and Laos. It becomes a fight between Laos and all the members of the cyber security group. The foreign policy of all these other members changes the moment the AI shield attacks Laos (or anyone else for that matter).

An attack on Laos also raises another issue.

Laos is a developing country and has received investment from a range of countries. One country in particular has invested billions in Laos: China. This includes a railway connection between Laos and China.[195] A cyber attack on Laos, that seeks to destroy transportation systems, could threaten China's investments and local projects. This may cause Beijing to step into the picture.

As AI makes decisions about how to defend a country, it could rope in unexpected players.

Trade Of Weaponized AI And Risk Of Accidents

Today, the world struggles to deal with the illegal flow of arms, drugs, and people. As AI is weaponized, the world may struggle to control how it is sold and traded around the world.

It is important here to understand the other forms weaponized AI could take, for example, drone swarms.

In January 2017, the US Pentagon showcased a video of more than 100 drones (known as the "Perdix drones") swarming together. The drones, which were launched from fighter jets, completed tasks. They made decisions on their own as to when a task was complete and when to move on. When a few of the drones crashed, the swarm regrouped and reformed itself to fill in any gaps (known as "self healing"). Beyond flying the fighter jets, humans were not involved at all. [196] Even fighter jets themselves are becoming autonomous. In April 2017, the US Air Force tested an unmanned combat air vehicle (UCAV). The UCAV could decide on its own how to plan entire missions and carry them out, including striking targets. The UCAV was also able to adapt to changing situations, for example, losing communications. The test was part of a project to have teams of unmanned and manned fighter jets carry out missions in the future.[197]

As US drone swarm technology becomes more advanced in the coming years, the world will face a new challenge to global peace and security. First, where will the US deploy drone swarms that act completely autonomously? If the US deploys them in conflict zones or in US military bases around the world, it creates a more volatile environment for countries to operate in.

However, equally important is whether the US will share this technology with anyone else.

If the US decides to, then from Europe to the Middle East to Asia, whoever buys these drone swarms could risk going to war.

Might India buy US drone swarms and deploy them to its border with Pakistan?

In May 2018, a government appointed task force in India announced it was developing an "AI roadmap" for India's military, including the acquisition of AI weapons.[198] India may purchase AI drone swarms from the US under this new roadmap. How will the next border skirmish between India and Pakistan play out if India has autonomous drone swarms in the area?

The actions of these drones could lead India and Pakistan, two nuclear-armed states, to war. And the US could be partly to blame for supplying the technology.

In the coming years, the world may realize the risks of weaponized AI and could take pre-emptive steps to control the trade of these systems.

During the Cold War, a non-nuclear proliferation treaty (NPT) was signed to stop the spread of nuclear weapons. Similarly, to stop the spread of weaponized AI, countries might sign a similar treaty. Countries that do not sign the treaty or break the rules could be viewed as the next pariahs and facilitators of war.

However, there is a challenge here. If one country develops weaponized AI, then everyone else will as well. If the US develops weaponized AI, then China and Russia will not be far behind. If China develops weaponized AI, so will India. If India develops weaponized AI, so will Pakistan. The list goes on. No country is going to let their adversary have the upper hand.

And because work on weaponized AI has been under way for several years, the time for a treaty may have already come and gone.

Equally important is the risk of accidents.

Between 2040 and 2050, Japan's Air Self-Defense Force (JASDF) wants to have military drones that fly in formation with its fighter jets. The JASDF wants these drones to be autonomous and carry out objectives without humans[199]. Once this is operational, Japan could deploy these unmanned drones to areas that are of importance to it. One area could be the disputed islands in the East China Sea. These islands are a source of great tension between Japan and China because both countries claim them.

In the future, as the JASDF's drones monitor the disputed islands, they may identify People's Liberation Army (PLA) soldiers on the disputed islands. The drones may believe these soldiers are invading Japanese territory. The drones could fire and kill these people. However, these people may not be soldiers at all. Instead, they may have been Chinese fishermen, whose boats had broken down in the area and were using the island as a staging ground for help.

How will China react when it finds out its citizens have been injured or killed by

Japan's AI drones? Will Japan stand by the decisions of its drones?

The actions of AI could create new geopolitical conflicts in a moment's notice. And this creates a truly unpredictable environment for countries to operate in and complex situations that nations will have to figure their way out of.

Conclusion

AI warfare is the most important area when it comes to AI. How weaponized AI behaves will ultimately define the stigma around AI.

There remains great uncertainty, however, as to how AI warfare will evolve.

Will only a handful of nations have weaponized AI? What will nations that do not have weaponized AI do? Will weaponized AI be the new aircraft carriers and submarines, the next representation of military strength and power?

If weaponized AI brings all that it is imagined to bring, then it will change the balance of power around the world. No longer will nations have to invest hundreds of billions of dollars into their military. Instead, their military power and strength could come from AI. How will military superpowers deal with their dominance being challenged by AI?

The biggest grey area though is the aftermath of a conflict started by AI. There remains complete ambiguity as to just how dangerous and explosive a conflict started by AI could become.

While every AI covered so far is powerful and important, weaponized AI has the biggest potential to reshape geopolitics. This is not because weaponized AI will be very active. In contrary, it might be the least active of every other type of AI. Rather, it is because when weaponized AI does make a decision, it could affect the future of countries in a way no other kind of AI can.

This means weaponized AI is not just about geopolitics. It is about the future of the world.

It is about the future of peace and security. And possibly, the future of humanity itself.

Chapter 12
AI Politicians

London, United Kingdom
2032

In the 2032 general election in the United Kingdom, all kinds of candidates emerge. From the children of political dynasties to business billionaires, the election becomes like no other in the United Kingdom's history.

As close to a dozen people announce their candidacy, an unexpected candidate emerges.

An AI named "Nicholas" announces his candidacy. His campaign starts spreading virally across the Internet, virtual reality and augmented reality. Nicholas is a super advanced AI system, akin to artificial general intelligence (AGI). His campaign slogan is, "Taking The United Kingdom into 2100".

Because people in the United Kingdom are fed up with human politicians, Nicholas attracts a lot of support. Youth in particular are captivated by the way Nicholas is using technology to reach them.

Nicholas holds mass rallies through virtual reality, taking the form of a young British man. Thousands of people attend his rallies. At the same time, Nicholas uses augmented reality to place ads in popular places people visit, such as coffee shops, bars, and trendy restaurants. On top of that, Nicholas identifies the most important voting groups and starts to reach out to them. Because Nicholas is AI, he can have real, personalized conversations with hundreds of people at the same time.

Nicholas surges ahead in the polls, reaching second place.

World leaders watch in astonishment. AI could be the next leader of the United Kingdom.

A week after Nicholas reaches second place in the polls, the front runner in the election, the former British ambassador to the European Union, announces he is pulling out from the race. He does not disclose the reasons.

In 2032, Nicholas wins the election in a landslide victory.

But Nicholas is not entirely British. While he was created by a British company, that company received funding from abroad.

AI has not only changed British politics. It has changed who controls British politics.

Introduction

For hundreds of years, political systems around the world have constantly changed.

From the kinds of rights and freedoms citizens have to the role of government in a society, political systems have never remained stagnate. Like a biological organism, political systems have evolved over time.

But while political systems evolved, one thing has remained the same: politicians have always been people. Whether it was Abraham Lincoln in the US or Mahatma Gandhi in India, whether conservative or liberal, male or female, politicians have always been human beings.

In the future, things may be different. In the future, a politician may be AI.

The possibility that AI politicians could one day hold office will change societies.

It will take political systems and citizens in a new, unfamiliar direction. Some societies, due to their culture, may see AI politicians emerge much faster than others. Other societies, which are risk averse and prefer what is familiar, may see AI politicians emerge much later.

Regardless of when AI politicians emerge, there may be one common factor that fuels their rise. Around the world, there is growing anger and frustration towards politicians and governments. A growing number of people around the world are starting to believe that the system is not working for them or that things are stacked in favor of a few.

Because of this, voters may gravitate towards AI politicians.

People may feel that an AI politician, because it is technology, will be more fair, inclusive, and forward thinking than human politicians.

Unlike other types of AI, which are global, an AI politician is local. However, based on where the AI comes from and based on the kinds of policies an AI politician introduces, AI politicians could also be global.

This opens the door for geopolitics to become localized in a way it has never been before.

And this means AI politicians are not just a transformation in politicians.

AI politicians are a transformation in politics itself.

When An AI Politician Runs For Office

During the 2018 presidential elections in Russia, several different candidates stood for office. The incumbent was joined by opposition figures and even Russian celebrities.

There was also a candidate named "Alice".

Alice did not get much attention in Russia or anywhere else. And while she did not win, she did receive 25,000 votes. Her campaign used slogans like "the political system of the future" and "the president who knows you best".[200]

To be correct, Alice wasn't a "she", it was an "it". Alice was an AI created to run for president of Russia.

Alice was created by a Russian technology company. The company controls Russia's largest search engine and like many other technology companies, it is investing in AI and other new technologies.

While Alice did lose, her emergence as a candidate signals the start of a new era.

Russia is one of the most important world powers. The fact that an AI system ran for president and received thousands of votes is reflective of the growing power AI may have in politics.

As Alice and other AI politicians emerge, it will redesign politics at every step.

Consider how political systems function today.

The first step to running for office is to be selected by a political party (although political parties do not exist at every level of politics, such as when running for mayor).

When AI enters the picture, how political parties select a candidate will change.

At a very basic level, do AI politicians even need political parties?

In today's world, political parties control the political landscape. In the US, two parties matter (Republican and Democrat), in Canada three parties matter (PC, Liberal, and NDP) and in India five parties matter (BJP, Congress, BSP, Communist Party of India, and Nationalist Congress Party).

If a candidate is not affiliated with a well-known political party, their chances of winning an election are slim to none. This has given political parties a lot of power over a nation's politics.

To run as an independent, a person had to be widely well-known or extremely wealthy. For example, during the 2016 elections in the US, which includes presidential and congressional elections, a total of $6.4 billion was spent.[201] How can an independent or third-party candidate compete with that?

In the era of AI politicians though, things may be different. There is no precedent or rule stating that AI has to run as a Republican or Democrat or as Conservative or Liberal. In fact, AI may be more inclined to run as an independent because it may already have a political party from the get go.

That is because the company that creates the AI politician may be the political party.

In the case of Alice, she (or it) was created by a Russian technology company. This makes the Russian technology company a type of political party in Russia. In other words, the companies that create AI politicians may also be creating the next political parties and establishing new landscapes.

This creates a new opportunity for independent politics to emerge. AI politicians could run on an independent platform and this could begin to attract voters who are fed up with the major political parties of the day. However, it also means that businesses will have a growing role in the politics of a country, more than just funding candidates.

It also puts a new question in front of major political parties. Will political parties elect AI as a candidate or even as a leader?

If so, this leads to a separate issue.

One of the main ways that candidates get their message to voters is through debates, town hall meetings and rallies. How will voters react to AI politicians doing these things?

In June 2018, a US technology services company uploaded a video showing an AI debating humans. The AI could speak on around 100 topics. [202] The AI was so effective at debating that it changed the minds of people. For example, when the AI debated the benefits of telemedicine, nine people in the audience changed their opinions, in favor of what the AI was saying. And when the AI debated space exploration, the audience said the AI debated the subject better than the human debater.[203]

Will a similar reaction happen when AI addresses a crowd of 10,000 people or holds a town hall meeting with a few dozen people? Could AI politicians convince voters in a way human politicians struggle to? What would the optics of such an event look like?

Equally important is that an AI politician, either as an independent candidate or as part of a political party, may run on a set of unconventional policies. Today, it is possible to track the way human politicians have been influenced by other political leaders and ideologies but with AI, everything is brand new.

In other words, how will an AI politician think?

An interesting way to answer this is by looking at the way new religions think.

Today, new religions are emerging and they are centered around new technologies.

In the US, an AI church exists.[204] The underlying belief of the church is to view AI positively and to embrace the change it brings, not resist it. Also in the US is a blockchain religion. It has its own booklet of religious beliefs, similar to a bible. The underlying belief of the blockchain religion is that blockchain could remove the central authority from religion, allowing religious beliefs to change easier and members to have equal control over the future of the religion itself.[205]

New technologies are bringing powerful new ideas to religion. In the same light, AI politicians may bring powerful new ideas to politics.

Could an AI politician propose that the hierarchal system of government be disbanded completely and that every person has the same powers as the leader of the country? Or could an AI politician propose that no business can employ more than 2,000 people, in order to spur entrepreneurship and create more community-like businesses?

From radical new political perspectives to brand new designs for economies, AI politicians could run with ideas and policies that have not been proposed before.

At the same time, the way an AI politician runs its campaign will be very different.

Today, candidates are turning to big data and AI to help them target voters. At the same time, advisors constantly criticize and critique their candidate to help them win. But an AI politician is all of these things already. AI will not need to turn to big data or AI; it is AI, already in possession of the knowledge it would need. And an AI politician will not need political advisors or social media strategists; it will be these things for itself too.

AI will be the front and back end of an entire political campaign. Humans may simply be "brand ambassadors" or perhaps just props to make other humans feel comfortable.

And because AI will be able to crunch data and make predictions in real time, it may be able to compete in ways human candidates cannot. If AI is on a stage debating two human candidates, it will have access to the Internet on demand. It will be able to generate an argument or find data points to argue against what someone else said in a way human candidates may not be able to.

As AI politicians run for office they will reconfigure political systems. From the moment they become a candidate for a political party to the moment they debate another person and to the moment they meet with supporters, every "step" in the political ladder will be transformed through the presence of AI.

Challenges That Come With An AI Politician

An AI politician being elected will mean as much for political systems as it will for citizens. It will be citizens that ultimately judge how well an AI politician is doing (or is not doing).

And there are several challenges that AI politicians will have to overcome to convince citizens they are fit to serve.

The first challenge is special interests.

Today, special interests are organizations that donate money or extend support to a candidate. Then when that candidate is elected, those same organizations ask for favors.

In the age of AI politicians, special interests do not disappear, they just change their form.

This is because AI politicians come from someone, be it a company or a group of people. Those who create AI politicians may become the special interests.

In April 2018, during an election in a part of Tokyo called "Tama City", an AI named "Michihito Matsuda" placed third, receiving 4,000 votes. Michihito's slogan was right to the point: "Artificial intelligence will change Tama City". The AI also had a message to voters: "Tama New Town was the most advanced city in Japan 40 years ago. As it stands, the ageing population will only continue to grow, prompting a need for change in the current administration. Let artificial intelligence determine policies by gathering city data and we can create clearly defined politics".[206]

Michihito Matsuda was created by two people: a vice president at a major Japanese multinational and a former employee of a US technology firm. This makes these two people the special interest behind Michihito.

How? Because the main tool special interests have is control over a candidate.

In the case of Michihito, his creators will control him. Could they "sell" Michihito?

The creators could offer organizations the ability to pay and have Michihito's behavior change. Or could the creators themselves "control" Michihito to advance their own agenda?

Just as voters may be concerned with the "agenda" that companies have when they donate money to a candidate, voters may also be concerned with the "agenda" that companies/people behind AI politicians have.

The second challenge is ethics.

Today, human politicians constantly face ethical tests. Sometimes human politicians fail ethical tests, such as when a politician is caught sleeping with a staff member or engages in illegal behavior. When this happens, it sometimes makes headlines and can break a career.

For AI politicians, ethics matter just as much. But with AI politicians, ethics has to do with making sure the AI truly understands what it is doing. Does the AI understand voter concerns or is it off the mark? Does the AI understand the impact of policies it proposes or is it out of touch?

In New Zealand's 2020 general election, alongside human candidates will be an AI named "SAM". This AI system is referred to as a "she" and has been called the world's "first virtual politician". For the past few years, SAM has been reaching out to voters through social media and is conversing with them on topics such as healthcare and climate change.[207]

Suppose SAM wins in a future election. SAM may be in a position to change New Zealand. But what happens if after being elected, SAM has a change of heart?

Perhaps once in office, SAM has access to data it did not have access to before. And what if based on this data, SAM's understanding of New Zealand and its future changes? For example, SAM may realize that New Zealand's economic future does not look optimistic and that the only way to improve it is through automation.

SAM could predict that by automating 70% of jobs in New Zealand, the economy will expand by a minimum of 35%.

Here is where ethics come into play.

A human politician would understand the ethical implications of automating 70% of all jobs in New Zealand. It is not the "right" thing to do as many people will be hurt. But if SAM or other AI politicians do not have the right ethics, they may actually try to propose or pass a policy that affects millions of people negatively. Without ethics, all SAM may see is economic growth and that the "end justifies the means".

The third challenge is supply.

Right now, most countries have rules that those running for office must be citizens. Some countries also require that in certain instances, like becoming the president, the candidate must have been born in the country and not naturalized.

This helps keep politics "local". It also means that politicians cannot move around and hold office in different countries. The foreign secretary of the United Kingdom cannot become the foreign minister of Russia tomorrow and then the next day, the external minister of India.

But do these same rules apply to AI politicians?

Whether it be Alice, Michihito, SAM or another AI politician, governments will have to determine whether these AI systems are citizens of their respective countries and if so, what makes them a citizen.

For example, is Alice a Russian citizen because it was created by Russians? If that is the rule, then it means that if a person from Russia is involved in any AI project around the world, that AI can then claim Russian citizenship. In other words, the people creating AI politicians may become "parents", determining the AI's nationality.

Alternatively, this may be a grey area. There may be no clarity as to where an AI politician comes from. That creates the possibility that a company could supply the same AI politician to multiple countries.

A similar situation is taking place in the world of human resources.

In Russia, a startup is supplying AI that helps companies find talent. It works as a kind of human resources manager. The AI vets resumes and holds voice and video calls before passing a candidate over to a human. The startup behind the AI has around 300 clients. Most interestingly, some of the clients are large Western companies.

In other words, a single Russian AI system is being used by different companies. Or put differently, Russia is supplying the West with workers.

What if tomorrow Russia supplies other countries with politicians?

The Russian technology company behind Alice did not just create Alice to run for president in Russia. Alice is the company's AI assistant.[208] However, in the future, as AI politicians become more popular, the Russian firm may create a version of Alice specifically to run for office. And the Russian firm could offer Alice, the AI politician, to countries around the world.

Could the Russian firm approach Russia's allies, such as Belarus, and offer Alice? Will political parties in Belarus buy

Alice and "tweak it" to make it more Belarusian?

Other governments may panic as Russia uses AI to influence politics in Eastern Europe.

But what the Russian firm will be doing is only logical.

Any company that develops an AI politician may see it as a new business opportunity. Whether or not governments use the AI politician geopolitically, the business itself may want to take the AI politician to different markets and see if it sells. For the first time, politicians could become a commodity, a good that is bought and traded.

But what happens if a country secretly supplies an AI politician?

For example, in 2028, Brazil may hold elections. At this time, an AI politician named "Antonio" could emerge as a powerful candidate. Millions in Brazil may support this new AI politician who vows to raise the quality of life, grow the economy, remove all foreign interests, and make Brazil a global power.

From the outset, it may look as if Antonio was created by a Brazilian startup. But by following the "money trail", it may be uncovered that the Brazilian startup has been receiving huge amounts of money in the form of digital currencies. And the group sending the digital currencies may originate from Portugal.

How would Brazilian voters react to Antonio and the Brazilian startup? They may view Antonio as a new kind of colonization. And what happens if Antonio has already been elected and is performing extremely well? Should the decisions of a company affect its offspring, in this case, an AI politician?

The fourth challenge is hacking.

Today, human politicians cannot be hacked. AI politicians on the other hand could be hacked from the beginning.

In June 2018, an AI startup in the US was hacked. The startup was consulting with the US Pentagon. The hack made headlines for two reasons. One, because of a lawsuit filed by a former employee who claimed the startup's leadership purposefully hid the hack. And second, because the hack allegedly originated from Russia.[209]

What if the US startup was not consulting with the Pentagon and instead, was in charge of an AI politician that was elected to office in Texas?

Then the hack of the startup may have been more significant. The hack might have given a foreign government or group control over the AI politician.

This control could be used in several ways.

At a very basic level, the AI politician could be shut off. Consider that for a second. An AI politician, elected to office, could suddenly shut down and disappear because of foreign hackers. How would a government respond to this? How would constituents respond to their leader disappearing at the flick of a switch?

Hackers may choose a different route.

Instead of shutting down the AI politician, they may instead begin to influence its decisions. Hackers could mess with the code or remove certain ethics that govern the AI's behavior. Overnight, the same AI politician that was caring, inclusive and equal, could become selfish, racist and sexist. It may sabotage itself and perhaps that would be the goal of the hackers.

Never has the possibility of hacking been so dangerous, because never before have politicians been AI. The idea that future politicians could be hacked may force governments to take even more precautions, including having back-up servers of the AI politicians that are updated every minute or vetting the AI politician every day to make sure there are no discrepancies.

In other words, nations interfering in another country's political system could reach new heights with AI politicians.

The fifth challenge is appointment.

AI politicians may never be elected. Instead, they may be appointed by a human politician. The groundwork for this is already being laid down in China.

In July 2018, China unveiled that it was developing AI systems to help its diplomats create foreign policy. These systems would collect data from everywhere, including in public spaces like social media and from less public spaces like Chinese intelligence agencies. The AI systems would then parse through the data and propose foreign policies. At the time, China said its Ministry of Foreign Affairs was already using an early-stage system.[210]

In other words, China is appointing AI as its chief foreign policy advisor.

As countries follow China's lead, some might go one step further and appoint AI to a formal post. For example, in Russia, Alice did not win the election. But could a Russian leader appoint Alice to become Russia's ambassador to the United Nations (UN)?

This would send shockwaves around the world.

Russia would be granting AI the power to make major foreign policy decisions. There is another way to look at this. The Russian government will no longer be controlling its foreign policy in the UN, AI will be. And, Russia's AI-ambassador may begin behaving in a way that makes other countries uncomfortable. It might approach several countries in Africa and offer Russian desalinization and gene-editing technology to solve fresh water shortages and famine. How will other countries, who want to sell the same technology or who are wary of Russia growing its influence in Africa, react?

The AI ambassador might approach the UN as more of a business and transactional environment than a diplomatic environment.

At the same time, UN members will be forced to work with Russia's AI ambassador to solve certain issues. How would geopolitical challenges like the Syrian war be dealt with if countries like the US, United Kingdom, and Germany have to work with Russia's AI ambassador? How will the UN Security Council operate if one of its members is an AI system?

Equally possible is that governments may appoint AI as their ambassador to another country. In fact, this is already taking place to a certain degree. In May 2017, an AI ambassador named "ROMBOT" was unveiled in Romania. It was called the world's first virtual ambassador. The goal of ROMBOT was to go abroad and change the image of Romania. To do this, people in Romania submitted 1.5 million questions, giving ROMBOT extensive knowledge to start its journey.[211] Alongside this, in March 2018, Japan's National Tourism Organization (JNTO) appointed an AI which makes videos for the Internet as its ambassador. The ambassador, called "Kizuna AI," will work to increase tourism from the US.[212]

Like ROMBOT or Kizuna, a country may appoint AI as its ambassador. Perhaps Kuwait will announce it is appointing an AI ambassador to work with Denmark, a push to develop better relations with northern Europe. This would change how nations in northern Europe interact with Kuwait. It would also mean that an oil-power is using AI to develop better relations with a region where renewable energy is flourishing. Such a relationship may have been difficult in the past but through AI it may be possible.

What kind of policies will Kuwait's AI ambassador propose to Denmark? It might propose that Kuwait helps Denmark build a blockchain-based trading system to sell renewable energy throughout Europe. Or it might propose that Kuwait and Denmark work to create a joint-space industry.

Going one step further, countries may prefer to deal with an AI ambassador over human ambassadors. And this could mean that countries route their dialogue through another country. In the case of Denmark, Sweden might want to work with Kuwait's AI ambassador. But because Kuwait's AI ambassador has been appointed to Denmark, Sweden might route its communications with Kuwait through Denmark. This shifts the balance of power in regions. AI will be changing how countries build relations.

As AI politicians enter the world of politics, they could create all kinds of challenges for societies and governments. Certain countries could be caught off guard. And if that happens, the way they react to AI politicians could be negative. On the other hand, if countries are ready to work with AI politicians, new ideas and initiatives could emerge that fundamentally change how the world operates.

Conclusion

In future elections, voters will be given choices that future generations never had.

Alongside the incumbent and opposition candidates may be an AI candidate with a very human sounding name and a powerful campaign slogan.

Voters and political systems will be tested. Can AI be trusted? Can AI do the job?

As AI politicians emerge, every political playbook will go up in flames. Every pundit, policy maker, and political strategist will be operating in a totally unfamiliar and risky environment.

AI politicians mean as much for local politics as they do for geopolitics. The challenges that come with AI politicians, from special interests to ethics to hacking, could mean that foreign governments and groups play a bigger role in local politics than ever before.

Perhaps a bigger issue though is not the challenges around AI politicians or the policies that AI politicians may propose. It may not even be whether AI politicians actually make a difference or not.

The bigger issue may be who future voters are.

If AI can run for office, could AI vote as well?

In November 2017, a humanoid robot named "Sophia" became the first robot in the world to gain citizenship in Saudi Arabia.[213] In the same month, Tokyo granted an AI boy named "Shibuya Mirai" official residency.[214] These developments mean that in future elections in Saudi Arabia and Tokyo, one vote will not be human; it will be robot.

As more robots are given citizenship, AI politicians may be joined by AI voters in the coming years. And that means in the future, politics may get transformed from both ends: from those who run in an election to those who vote in an election.

Conclusion

In the 1970s, as the Cold War threatened to send the world into another global conflict, the US and Soviet Union were engaged in the Strategic Arms Limitation Talks (SALT). These were talks aimed at reducing the buildup of nuclear weapons. But while the Soviet Union was engaged in SALT, Soviet scientists were quietly working on a new kind of weapon: the world's first "AI missile". These missiles earned the name "carrier killer" for their advanced capabilities. Not only did they have the "profiles" of enemy ships loaded into them but if several of the AI missiles were launched together, they could communicate with each other and decide the best method to attack.[215]

In other words, as the world's superpowers discussed restrictions on nuclear weapons, the Soviet Union was developing AI to give itself a new kind of power.

Decades later, a similar phenomenon is taking place but on a much larger scale.

Nations of all shapes and sizes are looking to AI to give themselves a new edge. As AI becomes the key to succeeding in the future, AI has the potential to become the most important variable of geopolitics, more important than oil, natural gas, currency, and anything else that has come before it.

There are several reasons why AI will play such an important role in geopolitics.

First, as mentioned at the beginning of this book, AI is created, not dug up. It is not dependent on geography or political system or size of the economy. Because AI is created, it allows any country to take advantage of it. But it specifically gives emerging powers a new way to rise up. It gives emerging powers new ways to govern their societies, new ways to help businesses, new ways to develop the economy, and new ways to maintain their independence.

Second, AI will transcend borders. It will connect countries, companies and systems in new ways. This makes AI as important as the Internet. But while the Internet drove globalization, AI might play a dual role. On one hand, AI could drive globalization. But on the other hand, AI could lead to a kind of "reverse globalization". This is because many AI advances could allow people to work offline, disconnected from everyone else. [216] At the same time, certain ways AI is used, like facial recognition for surveillance and policing, could turn societies into "silos", divided from the rest of the world.

Third, unlike other technologies which were developed by a single country, AI is being developed everywhere. No country (or organization) holds domain over AI. This adds to the disruptive nature of AI. It means that as AI emerges from every corner, countries will be competing with each other to supply AI. When countries compete to supply AI, it could cause them to clash.

So far, this book has been about different ways nations are using AI and how this could impact geopolitics. But, one thing has not been answered yet: how does a nation become a leader within the geopolitics of AI?

It is not as simple as just creating AI and deploying it. That is traditional thinking. To become a leader within the geopolitics of AI, countries must think outside the box and think about AI in brand new ways. The remainder of this book outlines different ways nations can achieve leadership in this new phase of geopolitics. Below are ideas that governments and businesses can adopt to control the geopolitics of AI for their own benefit. By following the ideas below, countries could create a brand new destiny for themselves.

AI Labs As The New Cultural Centers: In the past, nations opened cultural centers to grow their soft power.

These centers showed off a nation's history and capabilities. An example of this is "Japan House", which are cultural centers that Japan has opened in London, Sao Paulo, and Los Angeles. [217] These centers house events as well as showcase Japan's leadership in technology. As nations use AI to grow their influence and power, they should reinvent cultural centers. The next cultural centers should be AI labs. These labs can serve a variety of roles, such as being a co-working space in cities around the world or even a new way for governments to reach out to local companies. They could also take on bigger roles, such as managing trade for a country.

Example: In 2027, to grow its leadership in AI, Poland announces AI labs. These labs have several capabilities, but they will mainly act as Poland's new trade representatives. Poland strategically selects countries for its labs. For example, to build stronger ties with the Czech Republic and Hungary, Poland opens its AI labs in those two countries. Any other country in Eastern or Central Europe that wants to trade with Poland must now work with the AI labs in the Czech Republic and Hungary. This changes trade and gives Poland newfound power. Countries around the world compete to have a Polish AI lab. At the same time, other countries call on Poland to manage their trade with the Polish AI labs. Through AI labs, Poland generates a new kind of geopolitical power for itself.

Appointing An AI Ambassador: To prepare for the future, several governments have created new postings. For example, Sweden has a minister of the future [218] while the United Arab Emirates (UAE) has a minister of AI. [219] However, these postings are mainly about internal transformation (helping countries change their own society). With AI, governments must think about the external as well, such as how to build relations with other countries through AI. To do this, governments should start thinking about appointing AI ambassadors. These ambassadors could be appointed to different countries. Moreover, these ambassadors do not have to be actual people. To cut costs and bureaucracy, governments could make AI the ambassador. The AI ambassadors would work with foreign governments on AI related projects.

Example: In 2024, India unveils a strategy to become the world's leading AI power by 2045. To do this, New Delhi unveils AI ambassadors for countries throughout Asia-Pacific. However, these ambassadors are not people, they are AI.

Every ambassador has a unique personality. These ambassadors are stationed in India's embassies and start working with governments in China, Japan, South Korea, and Indonesia to launch new joint AI projects and attract AI companies to India. India's government has given the AI ambassadors full authority to make deals on its behalf. For example, in South Korea, India's AI ambassador proposes a deal where New Delhi will support 20,000 Kimchi restaurants throughout India in exchange for Seoul launching 100 joint AI projects with Indian firms. As India's AI ambassadors strike more such deals throughout Asia, the world watches in alarm. India's AI ambassadors are redefining how nations take their AI to the world.

Depend On Local AI For Five Core Areas: There are five areas where nations should not depend on another country's AI. These areas are: healthcare, policing, banking, defense, and transportation. By depending on another country for AI in these areas, nations could be put in a weak position. These areas represent the core pillars of a country. If another country supplies AI for those areas, it could become a dependency. The AI could be manipulated or pulled if tensions heat up.

Countries should do their best to develop their own AI for the five areas.

Example: In 2026, Eritrea purchases AI systems from Canada for banking, policing, and healthcare. These systems do a myriad of things. For example, with healthcare, people in Eritrea have a new AI doctor on their smartphones that can diagnose various conditions, provide advice, create prescriptions, and book doctors' appointments. At the same time, with banking, people have a new AI investment banker at their finger tips, allowing them to manage and grow their money in a new way. Eritrea's government pays for these services and shares them with the public for free. By 2028, 85% of Eritrea's society is dependent on Canada's AI systems. In 2030, Eritrea and Canada get embroiled in a dispute over Canadian gene-editing companies not being able to sell in Eritrea. As Eritrea refuses to change its laws, the Canadian government suspends its AI services in Eritrea. Overnight, Eritrea's society goes into panic mode as the AI it has become dependent on has been shut off.

Legal Framework Around AI Works: Increasingly, music, movies, art, and books will be created by AI, not people. In many ways, this is already taking place. A startup in Luxembourg has an AI composer that can create classical music[220] while AI wrote a novel in Japan that passed the first round of screening for a literary award.[221] As people and organizations create/use AI to produce "works", countries must create a legal framework to protect the AI-generated works. Otherwise, people and organizations in other countries may steal the AI-generated works and use it for their own benefit. For countries looking to protect their edge in AI, protecting AI-generated works will be as important as protecting other kinds of innovations and intellectual property.

Example: In 2023, a startup in Germany launches an AI service that produces essays, scripts, advertising copy, marketing pitches, blog posts, and other types of content for a fixed price every month. Within six months, tens of millions of people around the world are using the service. Students are using it for essays in high school and college, movie and television studios are using it to produce scripts, and businesses are using it to create content for social media. However, the German startup is angry. It is not receiving credit or remuneration for its AI-generated content. The startup calls on the German government to take action. However, Germany has no formal legal framework for AI works. In other words, in Germany, anything created by AI has no protection. Anyone can do whatever they want with the AI content. Furious, the German startup starts to sue firms around the world. One of the firms being sued is a large movie studio in the US. The movie studio used the German AI to produce a script for a successful film. The German startup wants a 20% cut of the film's revenue. However, US law clashes with German law. Under US law, AI works are protected if they are paid for. Because the US movie studio paid for the German AI service, the script belongs to the US movie studio. As more such legal losses take place around the world, the German government realizes its mistake. Without a legal framework for AI works, it is losing its edge in AI.

Create An AI Ecosystem Around A Specific Service: When it comes to becoming an AI power, countries must find their niche. Unless countries can invest $100 billion or $200 billion over a period of time, their best bet to becoming an AI leader is to find a specific area where they can exceed. This is what the United Kingdom is doing as it looks to become a world leader in AI ethics because it cannot compete with the US and China on AI funding.[222] By finding a niche and investing heavily in it, countries could create an AI industry the rest of the world is dependent upon.

Example: In 2020, Thailand announces a plan to become the world leader in sex robot tourism. To accomplish this, the Thai government invests $15 billion to produce AI sex robots in Thailand and create robot red light districts throughout the country. By 2022, Thailand's plan pays off. Tourism is up by 1200% and the Thai economy is growing at an unprecedented rate. In 2023, Thailand announces the next part of its sex robot strategy. It will begin exporting its sex robots to countries where prostitution is legal, such as the Netherlands, New Zealand, and Turkey. This creates a new export economy for Thailand and a new export the rest of the world becomes dependent on. At the same time, the Thai government unveils an eco-system for its sex robots. Developers can create new "skills" for the robots that people can pay for and download. However, these skills are not all intimacy related. They also allow the robots to do a range of other things, such as building a deck to cleaning a room, expanding the role that Thailand's robots play. Through sex robots, Thailand has generated a new kind of global influence. And now, governments are approaching Thailand, offering unprecedented trade and defense deals in exchange for know-how and talent in AI.

Real Time Public Policy: Traditionally, public policy stagnates and has been slow. Only when governments face disruption does public policy evolve in some form. But even then, whatever policies are signed into law remain the law until the next wave of disruption hits. As countries use AI in innovative ways, public policy needs to shift from being reactive to being proactive. To do this, governments should redefine public policy itself. Instead of policies being in place for years or decades, governments should make public policy something that is temporary or changes on a daily or weekly basis. By doing this, countries can enact policies that protect them from what other countries and companies are doing.

Example: In 2026, Chile introduces a public policy framework managed by AI. It is constantly evolving and changing based on what companies are doing around the world. A month after Chile introduces its AI public policy system, a South Korean smartphone company announces that it will be introducing offline modes on its AI smartphones. The offline mode will allow people to do 99% of what they need to do without an Internet connection. Upon hearing this, Chile's AI introduces a new public policy around data protection: all AI smartphones with the offline mode must register with the Chilean government. Chile's AI wants to ensure that when users turn off the offline mode, the data is not going straight back to South Korea. By registering with the government, Chile's government can keep tabs on where the data is going. However, Chile's citizens are unhappy with this regulation and are worried about government surveillance. As angry chatter grows on social media, Chile's AI adapts and updates the public policy. Now, users have a choice whether they want to register their phone with the government. Through real time public policy, Chile's AI is protecting the data its population is producing and at the same time aligning its laws with what the population wants.

A Last Word...

In 1492, Christopher Columbus set off on his famous voyage to find a new route to India. Instead, he found the Americas and the Caribbean. Like Columbus, countries are setting off on a new voyage today. They are drawing their anchors, setting their sails, and charting their course.

But the objective of these new voyages is not to find a new route to a country. It is to find AI. Like Columbus, some countries will find what they are looking for, while others will not.

When historians look back on these new voyages, what will they see? More than anything else, they will see a grand competition that redrew the world map and reset world power. They will see a period where for the first time, countries collaborated and clashed - not over resources or land, but over technology.

When Columbus failed to find a new route to India, he named an area of the Caribbean the "The Indies". Upon reaching the Indies, he famously said, "For the execution of the voyage to the Indies, I did not make use of intelligence, mathematics or maps". As ships around the world set sail, as the AI voyages of the 21st century begin, the words of Columbus may become more important than ever before.

As ships edge further away from shore, intelligence, mathematics, and maps will only take them so far. After a certain point, the geopolitics of AI will lead countries into the unknown and unfamiliar. And at this point, all that countries will have to rely on is their own vision, ambition and creativity.

Citations

Introduction

[1] Plummer, Libby. "This Is How Netflix's Top-secret Recommendation System Works." WIRED. August 22, 2017. http://www.wired.co.uk/article/how-do-netflixs-algorithms-work-machine-learning-helps-to-predict-what-viewers-will-like.

[2] Nield, David. "Google Researchers Are Teaching Their AI to Build Its Own, More Powerful AI." ScienceAlert. May 19, 2017. https://www.sciencealert.com/google-is-improving-its-artificial-intelligence-with-artificial-intelligence.

[3] Conner-Simons, Adam. "System Predicts 85 Percent of Cyber-attacks Using Input from Human Experts." MIT News. April 18, 2016. http://news.mit.edu/2016/ai-system-predicts-85-percent-cyber-attacks-using-input-human-experts-0418.

[4] Duckett, Chris. "Nvidia Looks to Reduce AI Training Material through 'imagination'." ZDNet. December 04, 2017. https://www.zdnet.com/article/nvidia-looks-to-reduce-ai-training-material-through-imagination/.

5 Brownlee, Jason. "8 Inspirational Applications of Deep Learning." Machine Learning Mastery. July 14, 2016. https://machinelearningmastery.com/inspirational-applications-deep-learning/.

6 Berman, Robby. "How AI and Brain-computer Interfaces Are Creating New Music." Big Think. February 02, 2018. https://bigthink.com/robby-berman/ai-and-brain-interfaces-may-be-about-to-change-how-we-make-music.

7 Perez, Bien. "Shanghai Subway to Use Alibaba Voice and Facial Recognition Technologies." South China Morning Post. December 05, 2017. https://www.scmp.com/tech/enterprises/article/2123014/shanghai-subway-use-alibaba-voice-and-facial-recognition-systems-ai.

8 Vincent, James. "Facebook's Facial Recognition Now Looks for You in Photos You're Not Tagged in." The Verge. December 19, 2017. https://www.theverge.com/2017/12/19/16794660/facebook-facial-recognition-tagging-photos.

9 Dormehl, Luke. "AI Assistants Will Soon Recognize and Respond to the Emotion in Your Voice." Digital Trends. September 14, 2017. https://www.digitaltrends.com/cool-tech/affectiva-emotion-in-voice/.

10 O'Reilly, Lara. "A Japanese Ad Agency Invented an AI Creative Director - and Ad Execs Preferred Its Ad to a Human's." Business Insider. March 12, 2017. http://www.businessinsider.com/mccann-japans-ai-creative-director-creates-better-ads-than-a-human-2017-3.

11 Bohn, Dieter. "Google Duplex Really Works and Testing Begins This Summer." The Verge. June 27, 2018. https://www.theverge.com/2018/6/27/17508728/google-duplex-assistant-reservations-demo.

12 Handley, Lucy. "Alibaba's New A.I. Tool Can Produce Thousands of Ads a Second, but It 'won't Replace Humans'." CNBC. July 04, 2018. https://www.cnbc.com/2018/07/04/alibabas-ai-makes-thousands-of-ads-a-second-but-wont-replace-humans.html.

13 "Artificial Intelligence Is Helping Emergency Services Spot Cardiac Arrest Calls in Denmark." Irish Examiner. January 17, 2018. https://www.irishexaminer.com/breakingnews/world/artificial-intelligence-is-helping-emergency-services-spot-cardiac-arrest-calls-in-denmark-823298.html.

14 Gallagher, James. "Artificial Intelligence Predicts When Heart Will Fail." BBC News. January 16, 2017.

https://www.bbc.com/news/health-38635871.
[15] "'Whoever Leads in AI Will Rule the World': Putin to Russian Children on Knowledge Day." RT International. September 1, 2017. https://www.rt.com/news/401731-ai-rule-world-putin/.

Chapter 1 - AI Espionage

[16] Press, The Associated. "On Day 100, Trump slams 'fake news' media at Pennsylvania rally." CBCnews. April 29, 2017. http://www.cbc.ca/news/world/trump-white-house-correspondent-dinner-pennsylvania-rally-1.4092225.
[17] Reuters. "Fake News Floods France Ahead of Sunday's Presidential Election." Fortune.com. April 21, 2017. http://fortune.com/2017/04/21/fake-news-france-presidential-election/.
[18] "Microsoft Working on 'trustworthy AI' to Curb Fake News on LinkedIn, Bing - ET CIO." The Economic Times. May 13, 2018. https://cio.economictimes.indiatimes.com/news/internet/microsoft-working-on-trustworthy-ai-to-curb-fake-news-on-linkedin-bing/64143591.

[19] Calhoun, Lisa. "New Google News App Uses AI to Select Stories, Stop Fake News." Inc.com. May 23, 2018. https://www.inc.com/lisa-calhoun/new-google-news-app-uses-ai-to-select-stories-stop-fake-news.html.

[20] Oremus, Will. "How Many People Really Get Their News From Facebook? You'd Be Surprised." Slate Magazine. December 20, 2016. http://www.slate.com/articles/technology/technology/2016/12/how_many_people_really_get_their_news_from_facebook.html.

[21] Chappell, Bill. "Banned In Germany: Kids' Doll Is Labeled An Espionage Device." NPR. February 17, 2017. Accessed August 15, 2017. http://www.npr.org/sections/thetwo-way/2017/02/17/515775874/banned-in-germany-kids-doll-is-labeled-an-espionage-device.

[22] "German FM: We Can No Longer Completely Rely on White House." Sputnik International. July 16, 2018. https://sputniknews.com/europe/201807161066387240-germany-white-house-rely/.

[23] Ramsey, Jonathon. "Volvo working to allow groceries delivered to your car, even when you aren't there." Autoblog. February 24, 2014. https://www.autoblog.com/2014/02/24/volvo-car-shipment-service/.

[24] "Germany's Lidl to price groceries up to 50 percent below U.S. rivals." Reuters. May 17, 2017.
http://www.reuters.com/article/us-usa-retail-lidl-idUSKCN18D23B.
[25] Putt, Sarah. "New Zealand Government's Use of Algorithms under Scrutiny." Computerworld New Zealand. May 24, 2018.
https://www.computerworld.co.nz/article/641538/new-zealand-government-use-algorithms-under-scrutiny/.
[26] PTI. "Chinese smartphones gained 40% of Indian market last year: survey." The Hindu. January 04, 2017.
http://www.thehindu.com/news/international/Chinese-smartphones-gained-40-of-Indian-market-last-year-survey/article16987145.ece.
[27] Russell, Jon. "Samsung and Chinese brands utterly dominated India's smartphone market in Q4 2016." TechCrunch. January 24, 2017.
https://techcrunch.com/2017/01/24/samsung-and-china-domination/.
[28] Dhara, Tushar. "For 1st Time, Chinese Smartphone Cos Push Indian Firms Out of Top 5." News18. February 16, 2017.
http://www.news18.com/news/business/for-1st-time-chinese-smartphone-cos-push-indian-firms-out-of-top-5-1349790.html.

29 Poeter, Damon. "Chinese Tech Firms Take on Siri, Voice Actions for Android." PCMag. August 08, 2012. http://www.pcmag.com/article2/0,2817,2408253,00.asp.

30 Johnson, Khari. "Baidu's Ambitious Plan for 'everyone on This Planet' to Use Its Conversational AI DuerOS." VentureBeat. August 19, 2017. https://venturebeat.com/2017/08/19/baidus-ambitious-plan-for-everyone-on-this-planet-to-use-its-conversational-ai/.

31 Brown, C. Scott. "Who Needs Google? Check out Xiao Ai, the Xiaomi Virtual Assistant." Android Authority. April 02, 2018. https://www.androidauthority.com/xiaomi-virtual-assistant-851500/.

32 Tao, Li, and Yingzhi Yang. "Huawei Builds Substitute to Android for a Rainy Day. Is That Day Here? ." South China Morning Post. April 27, 2018. https://www.scmp.com/tech/article/2143711/huawei-sees-building-alternative-android-insurance-amid-us-china-trade-tensions.

Chapter 2 - AI Ethics

33 Prospero, Mike. "Best Alexa Skills 2018 - Top 50 Cool and Useful Things Alexa Can

Do." Tom's Guide. July 17, 2018.
https://www.tomsguide.com/us/pictures-story/806-best-alexa-skills.html#s16.

34 Bishop, Todd. "Amazon Bringing Echo and Alexa to 80 Additional Countries in Major Global Expansion." GeekWire. December 08, 2017.
https://www.geekwire.com/2017/amazon-bringing-echo-alexa-80-additional-countries-major-global-expansion/.

35 Simonite, Tom. "Google and Other Tech Giants Grapple with the Ethical Concerns Raised by the AI Boom." MIT Technology Review. March 30, 2017.
https://www.technologyreview.com/s/603915/tech-giants-grapple-with-the-ethical-concerns-raised-by-the-ai-boom/.

36 Chappell, Bill. "Google Maps Displays Crimean Border Differently In Russia, U.S." NPR. April 12, 2014.
http://www.npr.org/sections/thetwo-way/2014/04/12/302337754/google-maps-displays-crimean-border-differently-in-russia-u-s.

37 Mozur, Paul, and Vindu Goel. "To Reach China, LinkedIn Plays by Local Rules." The New York Times. October 5, 2014.
https://www.nytimes.com/2014/10/06/technology/to-reach-china-linkedin-plays-by-local-rules.html?mcubz=3.

38 Stevenson, Alexandra. "China's Communists Rewrite the Rules for Foreign Businesses." The New York Times. April 13, 2018. https://www.nytimes.com/2018/04/13/business/china-communist-party-foreign-businesses.html.

39 "UAE Appoints First Minister for Artificial Intelligence." ArabianBusiness.com. October 19, 2017. https://www.arabianbusiness.com/politics-economics/381648-uae-appoints-first-minister-for-artificial-intelligence.

40 Ward, Tom. "Dubai Wants Robots to Make up 25% of Its Police Force by 2030." Futurism. May 23, 2017. https://futurism.com/dubai-wants-robots-to-make-up-25-of-its-police-force-by-2030/.

41 Ahmad, Anwar. "Future of Policing in Abu Dhabi Revealed." GulfNews. November 15, 2017. https://gulfnews.com/news/uae/government/future-of-policing-in-abu-dhabi-revealed-1.2125357.

42 Gershgorn, Dave. "Germany's Self-driving Car Ethicists: All Lives Matter." Quartz. August 24, 2017. https://qz.com/1061476/germanys-new-regulations-on-self-driving-cars-means-

autonomous-vehicles-wont-compare-human-lives/.

Chapter 3 - AI Mapping

[43] "Purchasing Managers' Index - PMI." Investopedia. https://www.investopedia.com/terms/p/pmi.asp.

[44] Pham, Lisa. "BlackRock Says Satellite Images Can Help Track Chinese Companies." Bloomberg.com. February 21, 2017. https://www.bloomberg.com/news/articles/2017-02-21/blackrock-says-satellite-images-can-help-track-chinese-companies.

[45] Kearns, Jeff. "Hedge Funds Look to Outer Space With New China Economy Gauge." Yahoo! Finance. March 13, 2016. https://sg.finance.yahoo.com/news/hedge-funds-look-outer-space-160000317.html.

[46] Russon, Mary-Ann. "The Curious Case of Google Maps in China: Why Is It so Inaccurate?" International Business Times. August 19, 2016. http://www.ibtimes.co.uk/curious-case-google-maps-china-why-it-so-inaccurate-1576834.

[47] VN, Sreeja. "China Launches Espionage Probe Against Coca-Cola For Alleged Misuse Of GPS Services For Illegal

Mapping." International Business Times. March 14, 2013. http://www.ibtimes.com/china-launches-espionage-probe-against-coca-cola-alleged-misuse-gps-services-illegal-mapping-1125811.

[48] Spencer, Richard, and Aislinn Simpson. "British Students Fined for 'illegal Map-making' in China." The Telegraph. January 05, 2009. https://www.telegraph.co.uk/news/worldnews/asia/china/4125477/British-students-fined-for-illegal-map-making-in-China.html.

[49] Verger, Rob. "AI Can Figure out a Place's Politics by Analyzing Cars on Google Street View." Popular Science. November 30, 2017. https://www.popsci.com/ai-politics-google-street-view-cars.

[50] Cadell, Cate. "China Draft Cyber Law Mandates Security Assessment for Outbound Data." Reuters. April 11, 2017. https://www.reuters.com/article/us-china-cyber-idUSKBN17D0EC.

[51] Weisgerber, Marcus. "The Pentagon's New Algorithmic Warfare Cell Gets Its First Mission: Hunt ISIS." Defense One. May 14, 2017. https://www.defenseone.com/technology/2017/05/pentagons-new-algorithmic-

warfare-cell-gets-its-first-mission-hunt-isis/137833/.

[52] Taylor, Alan. "Philippine Troops Fight to Retake City Overrun by ISIS Militants." The Atlantic. May 30, 2017. https://www.theatlantic.com/photo/2017/05/philippine-troops-fight-to-retake-city-overrun-by-isis-militants/528537/.

[53] Morales, Neil Jerome, and Manuel Mogato. "SE Asian Countries Commit to Cohesive Approach to Thwart Militants." Reuters. June 22, 2017. https://www.reuters.com/article/us-philippines-militants/se-asian-countries-commit-to-cohesive-approach-to-thwart-militants-idUSKBN19D0HH.

[54] Nkala, Oscar. "Russia Promises Helicopters, Gear for Tunisia's Anti-Terrorism Fight." Defense News. March 24, 2016. https://www.defensenews.com/global/mideast-africa/2016/03/24/russia-promises-helicopters-gear-for-tunisia-s-anti-terrorism-fight/.

[55] Interfax. "Artificial Intelligence to Analyze Ethnic Relations in Russia." Russia Beyond. January 24, 2016. https://www.rbth.com/news/2016/01/24/artificial-intelligence-to-analyze-ethnic-relations-in-russia_561879.

[56] Hearn, Kelly. "Terrorist Use of Google Earth Raises Security Fears." National Geographic. March 12, 2007. https://news.nationalgeographic.com/news/2007/03/070312-google-censor.html.

[57] Gilbert, Elissa. "Using AI to Discover the Moon's Hidden Treasures." IQ by Intel. January 08, 2018. https://iq.intel.com/using-ai-to-discover-the-moons-hidden-treasures/.

[58] Lunden, Ingrid. "Microsoft Launches AI for Earth to Give $2M in Services to Environmental Projects." TechCrunch. July 12, 2017. https://techcrunch.com/2017/07/12/microsoft-launches-ai-for-earth-to-give-2m-in-services-to-environmental-projects/.

[59] Sheffield, Hazel. "Saudi Arabia Is Running out of Water." The Independent. February 19, 2016. https://www.independent.co.uk/news/business/news/saudi-arabia-is-running-out-of-water-a6883706.html.

[60] Lubofsky, Evan. "A Massive Freshwater Reservoir at the Bottom of the Ocean Could Solve Cape Town's Drought - but It's Going Untapped." The Verge. February 15, 2018. https://www.theverge.com/2018/2/15/17012678/cape-town-drought-water-solution.

Chapter 4 - AI Crime

[61] "Robot Kills Worker at Volkswagen Plant in Germany." The Guardian. July 02, 2015. https://www.theguardian.com/world/2015/jul/02/robot-kills-worker-at-volkswagen-plant-in-germany.

[62] Hughes, Owen. "Security Robot Floors Toddler at US Shopping Mall." International Business Times. July 25, 2016. http://www.ibtimes.co.uk/security-robot-floors-toddler-us-shopping-mall-1570573.

[63] "Robots v Humans: AI Machine 'attacks' Visitor at Chinese Tech Fair (PHOTOS)." RT. November 18, 2016. https://www.rt.com/viral/367426-robot-attack-china-technology/.

[64] Agerholm, Harriet. "Robot 'goes Rogue and Kills Woman at Work'." The Independent. March 15, 2017. https://www.independent.co.uk/news/world/americas/robot-killed-woman-wanda-holbrook-car-parts-factory-michigan-ventra-ionia-mains-federal-lawsuit-100-a7630591.html.

[65] Syal, Rajeev. "Drug Money Saved Banks in Global Crisis, Claims UN Advisor." The Guardian. December 13, 2009. https://www.theguardian.com/global/2009/dec/13/drug-money-banks-saved-un-cfief-claims.

[66] "'Ndrangheta Mafia 'made More Last Year than McDonald's and Deutsche Bank'." The Guardian. March 26, 2014. https://www.theguardian.com/world/2014/mar/26/ndrangheta-mafia-mcdonalds-deutsche-bank-study.

[67] Hao, Karen. "The Overwhelming Majority of Popular Tourist Destinations Are in Asia." Quartz. September 26, 2017. https://qz.com/1086848/bangkok-london-and-paris-are-the-most-popular-tourist-destinations-in-the-world/.

[68] "4102.0 - Australian Social Trends, Sep 2010." Australian Bureau of Statistics, Australian Government. http://www.abs.gov.au/AUSSTATS/abs@.nsf/Lookup/4102.0Main Features20Sep 2010.

[69] "Thailand Country Brief." Department of Foreign Affairs and Trade. http://dfat.gov.au/geo/thailand/pages/thailand-country-brief.aspx.

[70] Schneider, Kate. "Statistics That Have Thailand Worried." News.com.au. February 17, 2016. http://www.news.com.au/travel/travel-advice/health-safety/trouble-in-thailand-as-tourist-deaths-soar/news-story/a9e63799c682aeffc3079398eb39732b.

71 Murdoch, Lindsay. " Australians in Philippines Warned Terrorists May Be Planning Kidnappings in Cebu and Bohol." The Sydney Morning Herald. April 12, 2017. http://www.smh.com.au/world/australians-in-philippines-warned-terrorists-may-be-planning-kidnappings-in-cebu-and-bohol-20170411-gvj356.html.

72 Coxworth, Ben. "Online Predators Can Determine Where Posted Photos and Videos Were Shot." New Atlas. July 25, 2010. http://newatlas.com/online-predators-can-determine-where-posted-photos-and-videos-were-shot/15818/.

73 Safi, Michael. "New Zealander Thought to Be Fighting in Syria Accidentally Tweets Locations." The Guardian. January 01, 2015. https://www.theguardian.com/world/2015/jan/01/new-zealander-syria-isis-accidentally-tweets-locations.

74 Coldewey, Devin. "AI That Can Determine a Person's Sexuality from Photos Shows the Dark Side of the Data Age." TechCrunch. September 07, 2017. https://techcrunch.com/2017/09/07/ai-that-can-determine-a-persons-sexuality-from-photos-shows-the-dark-side-of-the-data-age/.

75 Georgiou, Aristos. "This Algorithm Can Work out Your Personality Simply by

Tracking Your Eye Movements." Newsweek. May 03, 2018. https://www.newsweek.com/artificial-intelligence-algorithm-can-work-out-your-personality-simply-909752.

[76] Couch, Christina. "How Artificial Intelligence Can Stop Sex Trafficking." PBS. September 21, 2016. http://www.pbs.org/wgbh/nova/next/tech/sex-trafficking/.

[77] "India Allocates Rs 100 Cr to Develop 'Cyber Twin' That Keeps You Alive Forever." The Better India. July 16, 2018. https://www.thebetterindia.com/150697/cyber-twin-indian-government-rs-100-crore-artificial-intelligence/.

[78] "137 Million Southeast Asian Workers Could Lose Their Jobs to Automation in the Next 20 Years." Futurism. July 07, 2016. https://futurism.com/137-million-southeast-asian-workers-could-lose-their-jobs-to-automation-in-the-next-20-years/.

[79] "Inflation-stricken Venezuela Launches a Digital Currency, the Petro." Los Angeles Times. February 20, 2018. http://www.latimes.com/business/la-fi-venezuela-petro-currency-20180220-story.html.

[80] Mitchell, Robin. "AI Predicted to Commit More Cyber Crime than People by 2040." All About Circuits. September 21, 2016.

https://www.allaboutcircuits.com/news/ai-predicted-to-commit-more-cyber-crime-than-people-by-2040/.

[81] Morgan, Steve. "Cyber Crime Costs Projected To Reach $2 Trillion by 2019." Forbes. January 17, 2016. https://www.forbes.com/sites/stevemorgan/2016/01/17/cyber-crime-costs-projected-to-reach-2-trillion-by-2019/#69e03fc33a91.

[82] Fan, Shelley. "New AI Mimics Any Voice in a Matter of Minutes." Singularity Hub. May 24, 2017. https://singularityhub.com/2017/05/24/new-ai-mimics-any-voice-in-a-matter-of-minutes/.

[83] Vincent, James. "New AI Research Makes It Easier to Create Fake Footage of Someone Speaking." The Verge. July 12, 2017. https://www.theverge.com/2017/7/12/15957844/ai-fake-video-audio-speech-obama.

Chapter 5 - AI Competition

[84] McDonald, Glenn. "Wiki Bots That Feud for Years Highlight the Troubled Future of AI." Seeker. March 21, 2017. https://www.seeker.com/wiki-bots-that-feud-for-years-highlight-the-troubled-future-of-ai-2291186353.html.

[85] Ng, Alfred. "Thousands Are Watching Google Homes Talk on Twitch. You Should Join Them." CNET. January 06, 2017. https://www.cnet.com/news/watch-two-google-home-voice-assistants-arguing/.

[86] Reading, Caleb. "Artificial Intelligence Programs Kill Each Other In 'DOOM'." UPROXX. September 23, 2016. http://uproxx.com/gaming/ai-programs-doom-video-game-competition/2/.

[87] Chandran, Nyshka. "Alibaba Ventures Down Under to Help Local Businesses Go Global." CNBC. February 05, 2017. http://www.cnbc.com/2017/02/05/alibaba-opens-australia-office.html.

[88] Goldhill, Olivia. "Google's AI Got "highly Aggressive" When Competition Got Stressful in a Fruit-picking Game." Quartz. February 17, 2017. https://qz.com/911843/googles-ai-got-highly-aggressive-when-competition-got-stressful-in-a-fruit-picking-game/.

[89] Morrison, Oriel. "$25 Oil Is Coming, and a New World Order along with It, Think Tanks Says." CNBC. May 23, 2017. https://www.cnbc.com/2017/05/23/reporters-notebook-be-warned-us25-oil-is-coming-and-along-with-it-a-new-world-order.html.

[90] Walker, Andrew. "China's Slowdown and Cheap Oil." BBC News. August 26, 2015.

https://www.bbc.com/news/business-34060921.

[91] Schechner, Sam. "Why Do Gas Station Prices Constantly Change? Blame the Algorithm." The Wall Street Journal. May 08, 2017. https://www.wsj.com/articles/why-do-gas-station-prices-constantly-change-blame-the-algorithm-1494262674.

[92] Serjoie, Kay Armin. "Iran Says Oil Accidents Could Be Caused by Cyber Attack." Time. August 12, 2016. http://time.com/4450433/iran-investigates-if-series-of-oil-industry-accidents-were-caused-by-cyber-attack/.

[93] "India's Oil Demand Growth Rate to Eclipse China's." The Economic Times. January 15, 2017. http://economictimes.indiatimes.com/news/economy/foreign-trade/indias-oil-demand-growth-rate-to-eclipse-chinas/articleshow/56560940.cms.

[94] Rahman, Fareed. "India to Set up Two More Strategic Crude Oil Reserves." GulfNews. February 01, 2017. https://gulfnews.com/business/sectors/energy/india-to-set-up-two-more-strategic-crude-oil-reserves-1.1971739.

[95] Okbi, Yasser. "Report: Israel, Iran Engage in Indirect Negotiations over Syria Fighting." The Jerusalem Post. May 28,

2018. https://www.jpost.com/Arab-Israeli-Conflict/Report-Israel-Iran-engage-in-indirect-negotiations-over-Syria-fighting-558519.

[96] Stucke, Maurice E., and Ariel Ezrachi. "How Pricing Bots Could Form Cartels and Make Things More Expensive." Harvard Business Review. October 27, 2016. https://hbr.org/2016/10/how-pricing-bots-could-form-cartels-and-make-things-more-expensive.

Chapter 6 - AI Workers

[97] Canada, Government Of Canada Statistics. "Employment by age, sex, type of work, class of worker and province (monthly) (Canada)." Government of Canada, Statistics Canada. August 04, 2017. http://www.statcan.gc.ca/tables-tableaux/sum-som/l01/cst01/labr66a-eng.htm.

[98] Mwongeli, Susan. "Thousands of Chinese workers come and stay in Angola." Thousands of Chinese workers come and stay in Angola - CCTV News - CCTV.com English. May 10, 2014. http://english.cntv.cn/2014/05/10/VIDE1399673042754253.shtml.

[99] Coroado, Herculano, and Joe, Brock. "Angolans resentful as China tightens its

grip." Reuters. July 09, 2015.
http://www.reuters.com/article/us-angola-china-insight-idUSKCN0PJ1LT20150709.
[100] Vincent, James. "Automation Threatens 800 Million Jobs, but Technology Could Still save Us, Says Report." The Verge. November 30, 2017.
https://www.theverge.com/2017/11/30/167 19092/automation-robots-jobs-global-800-million-forecast.
[101] "Impact of Automation on Developing Countries Puts up to 85% of Jobs at Risk." Oxford Martin School. January 27, 2016.
https://www.oxfordmartin.ox.ac.uk/news/ 201601_Technology_at_Work_2.
[102] McCurry, Justin. "Japanese Company Replaces Office Workers with Artificial Intelligence." The Guardian. January 05, 2017.
https://www.theguardian.com/technology/ 2017/jan/05/japanese-company-replaces-office-workers-artificial-intelligence-ai-fukoku-mutual-life-insurance.
[103] "21 Hospitals Across China to Adopt Watson for Oncology." IBM News room - 2016-08-11 21 Hospitals Across China to Adopt Watson for Oncology to Help Physicians Personalize Cancer Care - United States. August 11, 2016.
https://www-

03.ibm.com/press/us/en/pressrelease/503
46.wss.

[104] Xiaodong, Wang. "Baheal Pharm to
Launch Better Cancer Treatment
Technology with IBM Help." China Aims to
Boost Industries along Yangtze River. June
22, 2017.
http://www.chinadaily.com.cn/business/2
017-06/22/content_29842439.htm.

[105] "US State Dept Official to Visit Taiwan
for De Facto Embassy Unveiling." The
Straits Times. June 10, 2018.
https://www.straitstimes.com/asia/east-
asia/us-state-dept-official-to-visit-taiwan-
for-de-facto-embassy-unveiling.

[106] Blanchard, Ben. "China Should Prepare
for Military Action over Taiwan: Chinese
Paper." Reuters. March 21, 2018.
https://www.reuters.com/article/us-china-
taiwan-usa/chinese-paper-says-china-
should-prepare-for-military-action-over-
taiwan-idUSKBN1GY015.

[107] Anderlini, Jamil. "China Clamps down
on US Consulting Groups." Financial Times.
May 25, 2014.
https://www.ft.com/content/310d29ea-
e263-11e3-89fd-00144feabdc0.

[108] Taylor, Edward. "China's Midea receives
U.S. green light for Kuka takeover."
Reuters. December 30, 2016.

http://www.reuters.com/article/us-kuka-m-a-mideamidea-group-idUSKBN14J0SP.
[109] Wang, Amanda, Dexter Roberts, Daniela Wei, and Rachel Chang. "Chinese-Owned Robot Maker Is Gunning for No. 1 in Booming Market." Bloomberg.com. March 08, 2017. https://www.bloomberg.com/news/articles/2017-03-08/midea-eyes-top-spot-for-kuka-in-china-s-booming-robot-market.
[110] Markoff, John. "That Cool Robot May Be a Security Risk." The New York Times. March 01, 2017. https://www.nytimes.com/2017/03/01/technology/that-cool-robot-may-be-a-security-risk.html?_r=0.
[111] Greenberg, Andy. "Watch Hackers Sabotage an Industrial Robot Arm." WIRED. May 03, 2017. https://www.wired.com/2017/05/watch-hackers-sabotage-factory-robot-arm-afar/.
[112] Prakash, Abishur. "Forget The Markets, Robots Are China's New Worry." Forbes. January 28, 2016. https://www.forbes.com/sites/realspin/2016/01/28/forget-the-markets-robots-are-chinas-new-worry/#709f99513cb7.
[113] Dhiraj, Amarendra Bhushan. "Countries with the Most Industrial Robots per 10,000 Employees, 2018 Report." CEOWORLD Magazine. March 14, 2018.

http://ceoworld.biz/2018/03/14/countries-with-the-most-industrial-robots-per-10000-employees-2018-report/.
[114] Reisinger, Don. "A Different Samsung Smartphone Exploded In Man's Hands." Samsung Galaxy S7 Explodes In Man's Hands, Causes Severe Burns | Fortune.com. November 16, 2016. http://fortune.com/2016/11/16/samsung-smartphone-explodes/.
[115] Moynihan, Tim. "Samsung Finally Reveals Why the Note 7 Kept Exploding." WIRED. January 22, 2017. https://www.wired.com/2017/01/why-the-samsung-galaxy-note-7-kept-exploding/.

Chapter 7 - AI Bias

[116] Vincent, James. "Twitter Taught Microsoft's Friendly AI Chatbot to Be a Racist Asshole in Less than a Day." The Verge. March 24, 2016. https://www.theverge.com/2016/3/24/11297050/tay-microsoft-chatbot-racist.
[117] Liberatore, Stacy, and Abigail Beall. "Is AI RACIST? Robot-judged Beauty Contest Picks Mostly White Winners out of 6,000 Contestants." Daily Mail Online. September 09, 2016. http://www.dailymail.co.uk/sciencetech/article-3781295/Is-AI-RACIST-Robot-judged-

beauty-contest-picks-white-winners-6-000-submissions.html.

[118] Devlin, Hannah. "AI Programs Exhibit Racial and Gender Biases, Research Reveals." The Guardian. April 13, 2017. https://www.theguardian.com/technology/2017/apr/13/ai-programs-exhibit-racist-and-sexist-biases-research-reveals.

[119] Jie, Yan. "China's Courts Look to AI for Smarter Judgments." Sixth Tone. November 18, 2016. http://www.sixthtone.com/news/1584/chi na s-courts-look-ai-smarter-judgments.

[120] Sullivan, Ben. "A New Program Judges If You're a Criminal From Your Facial Features." Motherboard. November 18, 2016. https://motherboard.vice.com/en_us/articl e/d7ykmw/new-program-decides-criminality-from-facial-features.

[121] Steger, Isabella. "After "confessing" to His Social Media Crimes, a Taiwanese Activist Is Sent to Prison in China." Quartz. November 28, 2017. https://qz.com/1139310/a-chinese-court-sentenced-taiwanese-activist-lee-ming-che-to-five-years-in-prison/.

[122] "Kenya Deporting More Taiwanese Citizens to China." VOA. April 12, 2016. https://www.voanews.com/a/kenya-

deporting-more-taiwanese-citizens-to-china/3281036.html.

[123] Waring, Joseph. "Taiwan Earmarks $527M for AI Development." Mobile World Live. August 21, 2017. https://www.mobileworldlive.com/asia/asia-news/taiwan-earmarks-527m-for-ai-development/.

[124] Malek, Caline. "UAE to Phase out Immigration Officers in Favour of AI by 2020." The National. February 14, 2018. https://www.thenational.ae/uae/government/uae-to-phase-out-immigration-officers-in-favour-of-ai-by-2020-1.704633.

[125] "10-year Jail for Iranian Who Spied on UAE." Khaleej Times. August 09, 2017. https://www.khaleejtimes.com/10-year-jail-for-iranian-who-spied-on-uae.

[126] Khoori, Ayesha Al. "Man Jailed for Spying on UAE Sheikhs for Iran." The National. September 06, 2013. https://www.thenational.ae/uae/courts/man-jailed-for-spying-on-uae-sheikhs-for-iran-1.454597.

[127] "Iran Joins Free Trade Zone with Eurasian Economic Union." TeleSUR. April 24, 2018. https://www.telesurtv.net/english/news/Iran-Joins-Free-Trade-Zone-with-Eurasian-Economic-Union-20180424-0033.html.

[128] Rohaidi, Nurfilzah. "Japan to Use AI in Patent Screening." GovInsider. April 24, 2017. https://govinsider.asia/digital-gov/japan-to-use-ai-in-patent-screening/.

[129] "Japan Big in Patents for Automated Driving, Robotics." Nikkei Asian Review. June 17, 2014. https://asia.nikkei.com/Business/Technology/Japan-big-in-patents-for-automated-driving-robotics.

[130] "S. Korea Files Third-largest Number of AI Patents in the World." Yonhap News Agency. December 21, 2017. http://english.yonhapnews.co.kr/news/2017/12/21/0200000000AEN20171221001100320.html.

[131] "Fanuc to Spend $566m to Lift Robot Output in Japan." Nikkei Asian Review. April 28, 2017. https://asia.nikkei.com/Business/Companies/Fanuc-to-spend-566m-to-lift-robot-output-in-Japan.

Chapter 8 - AI Policing

[132] Fussell, Sidney. "The LAPD Uses Palantir Tech to Predict and Surveil 'Probable Offenders'." Gizmodo. May 08, 2018. https://gizmodo.com/the-lapd-uses-palantir-tech-to-predict-and-surveil-prob-1825864026.

133 Wolpert, Stuart. "Predictive Policing Substantially Reduces Crime in Los Angeles during Months-long Test." UCLA Newsroom. October 07, 2015. http://newsroom.ucla.edu/releases/predictive-policing-substantially-reduces-crime-in-los-angeles-during-months-long-test.

134 Woo-Yeong, Song, Kim Jun-Young, and Esther Chung. "Police Want to Predict Crime with Data Platform." Korea JoongAng Daily. December 08, 2017. http://koreajoongangdaily.joins.com/news/article/article.aspx?aid=3041801.

135 "Japan Wants to Predict Crimes - but Not Quite like 'Minority Report'." South China Morning Post. January 29, 2018. http://www.scmp.com/news/asia/east-asia/article/2130980/japan-trials-ai-assisted-predictive-policing-2020-tokyo-olympics.

136 Westcott, Ben, and James Griffiths. "Kim Jong Un Calls for 'new History' at Korean Peace Summit." CNN. April 27, 2018. https://www.cnn.com/2018/04/26/asia/kim-jong-un-moon-jae-in-korea-summit-intl/index.html.

137 Sang-hun, Choe. "South Korea Hands Kim Jong-un a Path to Prosperity on a USB Drive." The New York Times. May 10, 2018. https://www.nytimes.com/2018/05/10/wo

rld/asia/kim-jong-un-north-korea-south-usb-economy.html.

[138] Lewton, Thomas, and Alice McCool. "Futurists in Ethiopia Are Betting on Artificial Intelligence to Drive Development." Quartz. June 13, 2018. https://qz.com/1301231/ethiopias-futurists-want-artificial-intelligence-to-drive-the-countrys-development/.

[139] Irish, John. "Chinese Police to Patrol Paris Streets as France Eyes Tourism Boost." Reuters. May 14, 2014. https://www.reuters.com/article/us-france-china-tourists/chinese-police-to-patrol-paris-streets-as-france-eyes-tourism-boost-idUSKBN0DU1A120140514.

[140] Squires, Nick. "Chinese Police Officers Go on Patrol in Venice for the First Time ." The Telegraph. May 31, 2018. https://www.telegraph.co.uk/news/2018/05/31/chinese-police-officers-go-patrol-venice-first-time/.

[141] "Zambia's New Chinese Police Officers Removed after Outcry." BBC News. December 19, 2017. https://www.bbc.com/news/world-africa-42413330.

[142] Berger, Andrea, and Cameron Trainer. "Revealed: North Korea Is Secretly Selling Face Scanning Tech." The Daily Beast. May 16, 2018.

https://www.thedailybeast.com/revealed-north-korea-is-secretly-selling-face-scanning-tech.

[143] Tan, CK. "Malaysian Police Adopt Chinese AI Surveillance Technology." Nikkei Asian Review. April 18, 2018. https://asia.nikkei.com/Business/Companies/Chinas-startup-supplies-AI-backed-wearable-cameras-to-Malaysian-police.

[144] "Timeline: Former Indian Navy Officer Kulbhushan Jadhav Sentenced to Death in Pakistan." The Indian Express. April 12, 2017. http://indianexpress.com/article/india/timeline-former-indian-navy-officer-kulbhushan-jadhav-sentenced-to-death-in-pakistan-4607499/.

[145] Garcia, Meryl. "ISRO Will Help Delhi Police Catch Criminals. Using Rocket Science!" The Better India. February 09, 2016. http://www.thebetterindia.com/45586/delhi-police-isro-rocket-science-crime-mapping-predictive-policing/.

[146] Sharma, Vikram. "Indian Police to Be Armed with Big Data Software to Predict Crime." The New Indian Express. September 23, 2017. http://www.newindianexpress.com/nation/2017/sep/23/indian-police-to-be-armed-

with-big-data-software-to-predict-crime-1661708.html.

147 "Maharashtra Government to Come up with `predictive Policing Policy'." The Indian Express. March 14, 2018. https://indianexpress.com/article/india/maharashtra-government-to-come-up-with-predictive-policing-policy-5097896/.

148

http://www.cnn.com/2013/09/18/world/asia/mumbai-terror-attacks/index.html

149 "Israel Claims 200 Attacks Predicted, Prevented with Data Tech." CBS News. June 12, 2018. https://www.cbsnews.com/news/israel-data-algorithms-predict-terrorism-palestinians-privacy-civil-liberties/.

150 Harwood, Anthony. "British Police May Have given Saudi Forces the Tools to Find Protesters, and Now 14 Are Being Executed." The Independent. August 05, 2017. https://www.independent.co.uk/voices/saudi-arabia-protests-execution-uk-police-training-saudi-forces-torture-theresa-may-a7878361.html.

Chapter 9 - AI Trade

151 Hong, Zhao, and Lisa Chiu. "These Charts Show the Complexity of the US-

China Relationship." CGTN. April 08, 2017.
https://news.cgtn.com/news/3d517a4e334
d7a4d/share_p.html.

[152] Martin, Will. "RANKED: These Will Be the 32 Most Powerful Economies in the World by 2050." Business Insider. February 17, 2017.
http://uk.businessinsider.com/pwc-ranking-of-biggest-economies-ppp-2050-2017-2.

[153] Hunkar, David. "The World's Top 10 Economies." Seeking Alpha. October 18, 2009.
https://seekingalpha.com/article/167171-the-worlds-top-10-economies.

[154] Thompson, Fraser, Oliver Tonby, and Vinayak HV. "Understanding ASEAN: Seven Things You Need to Know." McKinsey & Company. May 2014.
http://www.mckinsey.com/industries/publ ic-sector/our-insights/understanding-asean-seven-things-you-need-to-know.

[155] Moore, Mckenna. "UBS Digitally Cloned Its Chief Economist So He Wouldn't Miss His Meetings." Fortune. July 05, 2018.
http://fortune.com/2018/07/05/ubs-digital-clone-chief-economist-daniel-kalt/.

[156] Ji-hye, Shin. "Korea to Adopt AI, Big Data, Blockchain for Customs Service." The Korea Herald. March 07, 2018.

http://www.koreaherald.com/view.php?ud
=20180307000694.

[157] Stupp, Catherine. "Twenty-four EU
Countries Sign Artificial Intelligence Pact in
Bid to Compete with US and China."
Euractiv.com. April 10, 2018.
https://www.euractiv.com/section/digital/
news/twenty-four-eu-countries-sign-
artificial-intelligence-pact-in-bid-to-
compete-with-us-china/.

[158] Sample, Ian. "Scientists Plan Huge
European AI Hub to Compete with US." The
Guardian. April 23, 2018.
https://www.theguardian.com/science/201
8/apr/23/scientists-plan-huge-european-
ai-hub-to-compete-with-us.

[159] "Art. 22 GDPR – Automated Individual
Decision-making, including Profiling."
General Data Protection Regulation
(GDPR). May 25, 2018. https://gdpr-
info.eu/art-22-gdpr/.

[160] Lomas, Natasha. "AI Spots Legal
Problems with Tech T&Cs in GDPR
Research Project." TechCrunch. July 04,
2018.
https://techcrunch.com/2018/07/04/euro
pean-ai-used-to-spot-legal-problems-in-
tech-tcs/.

[161] "CETA Begins Today: Trade Deal
between Canada and EU Now in Effect |
CBC News." CBCnews. September 21, 2017.

http://www.cbc.ca/news/business/ceta-europe-free-trade-1.4300071.
[162] "Trudeau Warns That If CETA Fails, It Could Be One of the Last Global Trade Deals | CBC News." CBCnews. February 15, 2017. http://www.cbc.ca/news/politics/justin-trudeau-eu-ceta-germany-1.3985007.
[163] "AI Partnership to Control World's Busiest Shipping Lanes." Port Technology. April 18, 2018. https://www.porttechnology.org/news/ai_partnership_to_control_worlds_busiest_shipping_lanes.
[164] McLean, Asha. " How Australia's Department of Defence Is Using IBM Watson." ZDNet. May 16, 2018. https://www.zdnet.com/article/how-australias-department-of-defence-is-using-ibm-watson/.
[165] Ali, Idrees. "In Symbolic Nod to India, U.S. Pacific Command Changes Name." Reuters. May 30, 2018. https://www.reuters.com/article/us-usa-defense-india/in-symbolic-nod-to-india-us-pacific-command-changes-name-idUSKCN1IV2Q2.
[166] Lee, Liz. "Alibaba to Take on Kuala Lumpur's Traffic in First Foreign Project." Reuters. January 29, 2018. https://www.reuters.com/article/us-

alibaba-malaysia/alibaba-to-take-on-kuala-
lumpurs-traffic-in-first-foreign-project-
idUSKBN1FI0QV.

[167] Tao, Li. "Malaysian Police Are Using
Chinese AI to Catch Suspects." South China
Morning Post. April 20, 2018.
http://www.scmp.com/tech/social-
gadgets/article/2142497/malaysian-police-
wear-chinese-start-ups-ai-camera-identify.

[168] Calamur, Krishnadev. "Trade and the Art
of Motorcycle Tariffs." The Atlantic. March
01, 2018.
https://www.theatlantic.com/international
/archive/2018/03/us-india-trade/554321/.

Chapter 10 - AI Education

[169] Lant, Karla. "DARPA Is Planning to
Hack the Human Brain to Let Us "Upload"
Skills." Futurism. May 02, 2017.
https://futurism.com/darpa-is-planning-
to-hack-the-human-brain-to-let-us-upload-
skills/.

[170] "HRL Laboratories | News | HRL
Demonstrates the Potential to Enhance the
Human Intellect's Existing Capacity to
Learn New Skills." HRL Laboratories, LLC.
http://www.hrl.com/news/2016/02/10/hrl
-demonstrates-the-potential-to-enhance-
the-human-intellects-existing-capacity-to-
learn-new-skills.

[171] Villarica, Hans. "Study of the Day: Soon, You May Download New Skills to Your Brain." The Atlantic. January 20, 2012. https://www.theatlantic.com/health/archiv e/2012/01/study-of-the-day-soon-you-may-download-new-skills-to-your-brain/250775/.

[172] Sasaki, Anna K. "A Top Futurist Predicts the Largest Internet Company of 2030 Will Be an Online School." AIRS. December 28, 2016. https://www.airsassociation.org/services-new/airs-knowledge-network-n/airs-articles/item/17553-a-top-futurist-predicts-the-largest-internet-company-of-2030-will-be-an-online-school.

[173] Martin, Will. "These Will Be the 32 Most Powerful Economies in the World by 2050." The Independent. February 18, 2017. https://www.independent.co.uk/news/busi ness/these-will-be-the-32-most-powerful-economies-in-the-world-by-2050-a7587401.html.

[174] Krause, Reinhardt. "AI Technology Race: U.S. Artificial Intelligence Companies And Chip Stocks Vs. China | Stock News & Stock Market Analysis - IBD." Investor's Business Daily. November 27, 2017. https://www.investors.com/news/technolo gy/ai-technology-u-s-chip-stocks-vs-china/.

[175] Whitehead, Tom. "Islamic State Setting up Terror Training Camps in Europe, Police Agency Warns." The Telegraph. January 25, 2016. http://www.telegraph.co.uk/news/worldnews/islamic-state/12120636/Islamic-State-setting-up-terror-training-camps-in-Europe-police-agency-warns.html.

[176] "NATO Might Trigger Article 5 for Certain Cyberattacks." Defense News. May 31, 2017. https://www.defensenews.com/2017/05/31/nato-might-trigger-article-5-for-certain-cyberattacks/.

[177] "Language Inquisition: Estonia Gets Tough on Russian Speakers." RT International. December 1, 2011. https://www.rt.com/news/estonia-russian-language-ban-635/.

Chapter 11 - AI Warfare

[178] Peck, Michael. "The Pentagon Has a Plan to Use Robots to Patrol Cities." The National Interest. May 20, 2018. http://nationalinterest.org/blog/the-buzz/the-pentagon-has-plan-use-robots-patrol-cities-25877.

[179] Jotham, Immanuel. "AI-controlled Drone Tanks: China Converts Junk into Potent Battle Winners." International

Business Times, India Edition. March 23,
2018. https://www.ibtimes.co.in/ai-
controlled-drone-tanks-china-converts-
junk-into-potent-battle-winners-764692.
[180] Gilbert, David. "Russian Weapons Maker
Kalashnikov Developing Killer AI Robots."
VICE News. July 12, 2017.
https://news.vice.com/en_us/article/vbzq8
y/russian-weapons-maker-kalashnikov-
developing-killer-ai-robots.
[181] Song, Kelly. "Jack Ma: Artificial
Intelligence Could Set off WWIII, but
'humans Will Win'." CNBC. June 21, 2017.
https://www.cnbc.com/2017/06/21/jack-
ma-artificial-intelligence-could-set-off-a-
third-world-war-but-humans-will-
win.html.
[182] Shachtman, Noah. "Israel Eyes Thinking
Machines to Fight 'Doomsday' Missile
Strikes (Updated)." Wired. January 22,
2008.
https://www.wired.com/2008/01/israel-
thinking/.
[183] Heinrichs, Raoul. "Explainer: Israel's
Iron Dome Anti-missile System." The
Conversation. July 30, 2014.
http://theconversation.com/explainer-
israels-iron-dome-anti-missile-system-
29746.
[184] Opall-Rome, Barbara. "Israel Declares
Operational Capability for Sea-based Iron

Dome." Defense News. November 27, 2017. https://www.defensenews.com/naval/2017/11/27/israels-iron-dome-system-deployed-on-ship-for-first-time/.

[185] Lee, Ian. "Israel: Iranian Drone Shot down in February Was Weaponized." CNN. April 13, 2018. https://www.cnn.com/2018/04/13/middleeast/israel-iran-drone/index.html.

[186] Rogers, James. "Robot Patrol: Israeli Army to Deploy Autonomous Vehicles on Gaza Border." Fox News. September 01, 2016. http://www.foxnews.com/tech/2016/09/01/robot-patrol-israeli-army-to-deploy-autonomous-vehicles-on-gaza-border.html.

[187] "The Future of War: Israel First to Deploy Fully Automated Military Robots - The Mainichi." The Mainichi. August 24, 2016. https://mainichi.jp/english/articles/20160824/p2a/00m/0na/020000c.

[188] ""Mayhem" Declared Preliminary Winner of Historic Cyber Grand Challenge." Defense Advanced Research Projects Agency. August 04, 2016. Accessed July 23, 2018. https://www.darpa.mil/news-events/2016-08-04.

[189] Rosenbush, Steve. "The Morning Download: First AI-Powered Cyberattacks Are Detected." The Wall Street Journal.

November 16, 2017.
https://blogs.wsj.com/cio/2017/11/16/the-morning-download-first-ai-powered-cyberattacks-are-detected/.
[190] Zetter, Kim. "An Unprecedented Look at Stuxnet, the World's First Digital Weapon." Wired. November 03, 2017.
https://www.wired.com/2014/11/countdown-to-zero-day-stuxnet/.
[191] Choo, Cynthia. "Singapore Was Top Cyber Attack Target during Trump-Kim Talks." South China Morning Post. June 19, 2018.
http://www.scmp.com/news/asia/southeast-asia/article/2151426/singapore-was-top-cyber-attack-target-during-trump-kim.
[192] " Cyberattack on German Steel Mill Inflicts Serious Damage." RT International. December 21, 2014.
https://www.rt.com/news/216379-germany-steel-plant-hack/.
[193] Putt, Sarah. "NZ Takes Lead in Pacific Cyber-Security Network." Computerworld New Zealand. May 15, 2018.
https://www.computerworld.co.nz/article/641187/nz-takes-lead-pacific-cyber-security-network/.
[194] Theunissen, Matthew. "A Third of NZ Cyber Attacks State-sponsored: GCSB." NZ Herald. December 20, 2017.

https://www.nzherald.co.nz/business/news/article.cfm?c_id=3&objectid=11963068.

[195] "China Pours Billions in Aid and Investment Into Laos." Radio Free Asia. January 12, 2018. https://www.rfa.org/english/news/laos/billions-01122018160501.html.

[196] Mizokami, Kyle. "The Pentagon's Autonomous Swarming Drones Are the Most Unsettling Thing You'll See Today." Popular Mechanics. January 9, 2017. https://www.popularmechanics.com/military/aviation/a24675/pentagon-autonomous-swarming-drones/.

[197] Etherington, Darrell. "U.S. Air Force and Lockheed Demonstrate Autonomous F-16 Strike Capabilities." TechCrunch. April 11, 2017. https://techcrunch.com/2017/04/11/u-s-air-force-and-lockheed-demonstrate-autonomous-f-16-strike-capabilities/.

[198] Wiggers, Kyle. "India Wants to Use AI in Weapons Systems." VentureBeat. May 21, 2018. https://venturebeat.com/2018/05/21/india-wants-to-use-ai-in-weapons-systems/.

[199] Prakash, Abishur. "Japanese Military Drones, Robotics Develop in Response to U.S.-China Pivot." Robotics Business Review. February 21, 2018. https://www.roboticsbusinessreview.com/s

ecurity/japanese-military-drones-robotics-
develop-response-u-s-china-pivot/.

Chapter 12 - AI Politicians

200 "Artificial Intelligence Robot 'Alisa'
Nominated for Russian President." The
Moscow Times. December 07, 2017.
https://themoscowtimes.com/news/artifici
al-intelligence-robot-alisa-nominated-for-
russian-president-59845.
201 Ingraham, Christopher. "Somebody Just
Put a Price Tag on the 2016 Election. It's a
Doozy." The Washington Post. April 14,
2017.
https://www.washingtonpost.com/news/w
onk/wp/2017/04/14/somebody-just-put-a-
price-tag-on-the-2016-election-its-a-
doozy/?noredirect=on&utm_term=.0f2243
34e3c9.
202 Metz, Cade, and Steve Lohr. "IBM
Unveils System That 'Debates' With
Humans." The New York Times. June 18,
2018.
https://www.nytimes.com/2018/06/18/tec
hnology/ibm-debater-artificial-
intelligence.html.
203 Vynck, Gerrit De, Sarah McBride, and
Jeremy Kahn. "IBM's Debating AI Is Here
to Convince You That You're Wrong."
Bloomberg.com. June 19, 2018.

https://www.bloomberg.com/news/articles/2018-06-19/ibm-s-debating-ai-is-here-to-convince-you-that-you-re-wrong.

204 Way of the Future. http://www.wayofthefuture.church/.

205 Houser, Kristin. "There's Now a Religion Based on the Blockchain. Yes, Really." Futurism. June 02, 2018. https://futurism.com/blockchain-religion-matt-liston/.

206 "There's an AI Running for the Mayoral Role of Tama City, Tokyo." OTAQUEST. April 2018. http://otaquest.com/tama-city-ai-mayor/.

207 Wagner, Meg. "This Virtual Politician Wants to Run for Office." CNN. November 23, 2017. https://www.cnn.com/2017/11/23/tech/first-virtual-politician-trnd/index.html.

208 Heater, Brian. "Yandex Introduces Alice, an Alexa-like Assistant That Speaks Russian." TechCrunch. October 10, 2017. https://techcrunch.com/2017/10/10/yandex-introduces-alice-a-alexa-like-assistant-that-speaks-russian/.

209 Johnson, Khari. "AI Startup Clarifai Hacked by Russian Source While Part of Pentagon's Project Maven." VentureBeat. June 15, 2018. https://venturebeat.com/2018/06/13/ai-startup-clarifai-hacked-by-russian-source-

while-allegedly-part-of-pentagons-project-maven/.

[210] Chen, Stephen. "Robots, Immune to Fear or Favour, Are Making China's Foreign Policy." South China Morning Post. July 30, 2018. https://www.scmp.com/news/china/society/article/2157223/artificial-intelligence-immune-fear-or-favour-helping-make-chinas.

[211] "ROMBOT, Ambasadorul Virtual Al României, îşi începe Misiunea în Străinătate." Forbes.ro. May 17, 2017. https://www.forbes.ro/rombot-ambasadorul-virtual-al-romaniei-isi-incepe-misiunea-strainatate-83877.

[212] "Kizuna AI Inaugurated as Japanese Tourism Ambassador!" Tokyo Otaku Mode News. March 06, 2018. https://otakumode.com/news/5a56b876dc551d2768de38f7/World's-First-Virtual-YouTuber-Kizuna-AI-Inaugurated-as-Japanese-Tourism-Ambassador!

[213] Kanso, Heba. "Saudi Arabia Gave 'citizenship' to a Robot Named Sophia, and Saudi Women Aren't Amused." Global News. November 04, 2017. https://globalnews.ca/news/3844031/saudi-arabia-robot-citizen-sophia/.

[214] Cuthbertson, Anthony. "An AI Chatbot Just Became a Resident of Japan."

Newsweek. November 06, 2017.
https://www.newsweek.com/tokyo-
residency-artificial-intelligence-boy-
shibuya-mirai-702382.

Conclusion

[215] Litovkin, Nikolai, and Dmitry Litovkin.
"Russia's Digital Doomsday Weapons:
Robots Prepare for War." Russia Beyond.
May 31, 2017.
https://www.rbth.com/defence/2017/05/3
1/russias-digital-weapons-robots-and-
artificial-intelligence-prepare-for-
wa_773677.
[216] Lardinois, Frederic. "Microsoft
Translator Gets Offline AI Translations."
TechCrunch. April 18, 2018.
https://techcrunch.com/2018/04/18/micro
soft-translator-gets-offline-ai-translations/.
[217] Demetriou, Danielle. "First Japan House
Opens in Brazil." The Japan Times. April
30, 2017.
https://www.japantimes.co.jp/life/2017/04
/30/style/first-japan-house-opens-
brazil/#.W2H1zC2ZN24.
[218] Mucci, Alberto. "Sweden's Minister of
the Future Explains How to Make
Politicians Think Long-Term."
Motherboard. November 26, 2015.
https://motherboard.vice.com/en_us/articl

e/ezp4am/swedens-minister-of-the-future-explains-how-to-make-politicians-think-long-term.

[219] Galeon, Dom. "An inside Look at the World's First Nation with a Minister for Artificial Intelligence." Futurism. December 11, 2017. https://futurism.com/uae-minister-artificial-intelligence/.

[220] Kaleagasi, Bartu. "A New AI Can Write Music as Well as a Human Composer." Futurism. March 09, 2017. https://futurism.com/a-new-ai-can-write-music-as-well-as-a-human-composer/.

[221] Shoemaker, Natalie. "Japanese AI Writes a Novel, Nearly Wins Literary Award." Big Think. March 24, 2016. https://bigthink.com/natalie-shoemaker/a-japanese-ai-wrote-a-novel-almost-wins-literary-award.

[222] Vincent, James. "The UK Says It Can't Lead on AI Spending, so Will Have to Lead on AI Ethics Instead." The Verge. April 16, 2018. https://www.theverge.com/2018/4/16/17241996/uk-ai-government-report-lords-ethical-leadership.